"...BUT GOD!"

True Stories About God's Love, Mercy, Grace, and Intervention

Rev. Dr. Karen Joy King

WESTBOW
PRESS
A DIVISION OF THOMAS NELSON
& ZONDERVAN

Scripture taken from the New King James Version. Copyright 1979, 1980, 1982 by Thomas Nelson, inc. Used by permission. All rights reserved.

Author Credits: ". . . But God" is a blessing to read! It truly shows that God is interested in every detail of our lives and is an ever present help in the time of need. Walk with Him every day so that when you have a particular need, you know how to call upon Him.

WestBow Press books may be ordered through booksellers or by contacting:

WestBow Press
A Division of Thomas Nelson & Zondervan
1663 Liberty Drive
Bloomington, IN 47403
www.westbowpress.com
1 (866) 928-1240

ISBN: 978-1-4908-4638-5 (sc)

Library of Congress Control Number: 2014913552

Printed in the United States of America.

WestBow Press rev. date: 08/05/2014

Contents

Dedication ix

Introduction xi

About the Cover xv

About the Cover Artist xix

About the Illustrator xxiii

1. The Impossible Becomes Possible Through God ... 1

2. The Smoking Habit Broken 11

3. Jesus Wouldn't Let Go 14

4. Poor Boy Gets Shoes 17

5. God Lifted My Burden 20

6. God Lifted Another Burden 23

7. Jesus Stills the Storm 26

8. Stubborn Table – Thank God It Was Stubborn! ... 28

9. The First Time I Saw God Smile at Me 34

10. An Angel Drove My Car 37

11. Another Angel Incident 40

12. Desperate at Gas Station 42

13. Don't Waste Your Pain 46

14. My Journey With God 54

15. The Little White Bible 59

16. Will You Forgive Him? 69

17. I Completed 10 University Courses in
    Less Than 3 Months 79

18. My Gift From God 84

19. It Pays to Listen and Obey 89

20. The Stained Glass Window 93

21. A Fire Forced Us From Our Home 97

22. Father, Take the Wheel 103

23. "I Want You to Brush His Hair" 108

24. Isn't It Amazing? 118

25. The Sword Was Pulled Out of Her Back 123

26. Piano Teacher Healed 130

27. God Provided for Two Houses 132

28. Technically Challenged 137

29. God's Answer to Prayer 140

30. Believe it or Not, There is a Devil 143

31. The Hope We Have in Christ 149

32. Waking Up Depressed on Sundays 153

33. David and Goliath...156

34. Received a Husband and a House
    Through Prayer.. 162

35. God Kept Her Home... 165

36. God Knew the Truth 168

37. The Reunion 173

38. God Supplied the New Roof and Siding........... 179

39. Does Jesus Care?.. 183

40. From a Prisoner to a Ruler
    (The Troublesome Coats).................................. 188

41. This Was Not in My Plans – Not in a
    Million Years!...197

42. She No Longer Worries About Her Bills 203

43. An Angel Saved My Life...................................207

44. Death Was Cheated 211

45. We Needed a Special Miracle........................... 216

46. God Has a Plan for My Life 229

Epilogue 231

Appendix...235

Dedication

I wish to dedicate this book to:

*My wonderful friends, Christian Leadership University faculty and students, and even strangers who have richly blessed me by providing many of these ". . . But God!" stories.

*My daughter, Rachel Johnson, who encouraged me to finish this book and get it published.

*My good friends, Char and Cherie for proof reading and encouraging me.

*Most of all, God, Who prompted me to write this book.

"He's Got the Whole World in His Hands" and
that includes you and me!

Introduction

Psalm 66:10-12 "For You, have tested us. You have refined us as silver is refined and purified. You brought us into the net. You laid affliction on our backs. You have caused men to ride over our heads. We went through fire and through water; but You (". . . But God!") brought us out to rich fulfillment (abundance, refreshment)."

". . . But God!" is the first book I have attempted to write, although I have written many papers as a student and articles as a university professor and local newspaper reporter. God first laid it on my heart in 2010 by giving me the title only. In 2011, He gave me the cover design and finally the contents. So I began collecting these inspirational, real-life stories and writing them up.

I was almost finished writing ". . . But God!" when God led me to start and pastor a church, New Beginnings Ministries of Fayette, Ohio, in 2012. Due to the new pastoral responsibilities, the ". . . But

God!" writing stopped until April 2014 when friends, family, and God prompted me to finish it and have it published.

Since this is God's book through me to you, I pray that it will greatly bless you and help you better know our wonderful God Who created the universe and yet chooses to dwell within those who accept Him as their Savior. It is written simply and from my heart as God gave it to me. Each story is real – no fiction here.

The stories and teachings come from my life, my students, various friends and acquaintances, the Bible (stories which I have paraphrased), from some books I have read, and a variety of other sources. Some are very short, some are more involved and longer, some are just little reminders of God's goodness and how to handle problems, and some are teachings which I hope are helpful. Actually, no one has to look very far to find a ". . . But God" experience for God is always working in our lives.

It is my prayer that each experience and teaching will show you how much God loves and cares for you and that He answers when you call out to Him. Jeremiah 33:3, "Call unto me, and I will answer you and show you great and mighty things which you do not know."

About the Cover

God gave me a vision of the cover before I knew what the book content was to be. He told me the cover background should be a colorful universe which portrays His magnitude and beauty. Jesus holding the earth indicates that He is always watching over us, even though we may not realize it, and that He is an ever present help in the time of need.

He is eternal, without beginning or end. He is all knowing and powerful yet lovingly holds us in His Hand. His smile indicates His love for His creation, especially mankind who is created in His own image.

Below are a few supporting scriptures for above statements.

Genesis 1:1, "In the beginning God created the heavens and the earth."

Genesis 2:7, "And the Lord God formed man of the dust of the ground, and breathed into his nostrils the breath of life; and man became a living being."

Isaiah 41:10, "Do not fear, for I am with you; do not anxiously look about you, for I am your God. I will strengthen you, surely I will help you. Surely I will uphold you with My righteous right hand."

Isaiah 41:13, "For I am the Lord your God Who upholds your right hand Who says to you, 'Do not fear, I will help you."

Isaiah 48:13, "Surely My hand formed the earth, and My right hand spread out the heavens; When I call to them, they stand together."

Isaiah 49:15, 16a – Can a woman forget her nursing child and have no compassion on the son/daughter of her womb? Even these may forget, but I will not forget you. Behold, I have inscribed you on the palms of My hands.

Isaiah 49:1b-2a, "The Lord called me from the womb; from the body of my mother He named me, He made my mouth like a sharp sword, in the shadow of His hand He concealed me."

Isaiah 66:2: "For My hand made all these things, thus all these things (heaven and earth) came into being, declared the Lord."

John 3:16, "For God so loved the world that He gave His only begotten Son, that whosoever believes in Him shall not perish, but have eternal life."

About the Cover Artist

Bobbi Schlosser is a Training Specialist for an Art Department at a facility for Special Needs people. She has worked with these wonderful people for eighteen years and sees this as a ministry. There is no doubt in Bobbi's mind that her Heavenly Father placed her there since it allows her to use her God-given painting gift to teach the disabled the wonderful world of art. She is an accomplished artist and has won numerous awards. She also serves as a Senior Center facility supervisor and is the proud grandmother of seven grandchildren. In her spare time, she is an active member of the Black Swamp Art Guild of Williams County, Ohio.

Bobbi has recently authored and illustrated a children's book entitled "Pilgrim" which is about a black and white cat that got its head stuck in a tin can. Fortunately for the cat, Bobbi found it along the road while driving to work one morning. Since the rescue took place two days before Thanksgiving, she named it

"Pilgrim." The book "Pilgrim – A True Story," by Bobbi Schlosser, can be purchased through www.amazon.com Trafford Publishing, Bloomington, Indiana. It is also available at Special Occasions in Bryan, Ohio for $14.00. "Pilgrim" is a very cute book with fantastic paintings of Bobbi's dog and Pilgrim. The story is a simple message about kindness and would make a great gift for both children and adults!

Doing the cover painting is a ". . . But God!" story for Bobbi. When Bobbi told her Pastor, Nick Woodall, about painting the cover for Karen Joy King's book ". . . But God!" he was very happy for both her and Karen. He affirmed this was a calling from God for Bobbi since the last few months were very difficult for her due to losing the love of her life to cancer -- her husband of 45 years. After his passing, she hadn't been able to pick up a paint brush until now.

Bobbi Schlosser working at one of paintings.
Bobbi has won numerous awards for her paintings.

It was a miracle for Karen's and Bobbi's paths to cross at this particular time; for Karen needed an artist to do the special cover design God had given her and Bobbi needed to use her God-given painting talent again. They had never met until a mutual friend, Rebecca Lovelass, found out their needs and got them together for this project. ". . . But God!"

About the Illustrator

The illustrations for ". . . But God!" were drawn and colored by my granddaughter, Heidi Smith. Heidi has many interests and one of them is to become a professional illustrator.

This is her first attempt at drawing illustrations for a book. I call her my "budding" artist! It will be interesting to compare these illustrations with her future ones.

Heidi Lynnea Smith with her doll Samantha.
Notice their matching outfits.

With men this is impossible,

but with God all things are possible.

Matthew 19:26 NKJV

1. <u>The Impossible Becomes Possible Through God</u>

<u>(Paraphrased from Genesis 12-22)</u>

(By Karen Joy King)

God. . . Do you personally know Him, or is He some big mystery to you? Maybe you don't even believe in God, or maybe you call something or someone else your god. As you read this book, I hope to prove to you there is a personal God Who created you, loves you, and is always present with you.

From time to time, I will be taking stories from the Bible to show how God worked with people a long time ago. Keep in mind they were just as real and human as we are today. If God could do special things for them, He can do them for you. I would like to start with the story of the impossible child and how through God, Abraham and Sarah birthed him.

God called Abram, at the age of 75 (an age most of us would be settled back and taking life easy), to leave his home land and family and go to a new land. Abram obediently followed God into the foreign country with his wife Sarai. God promised Abram He would greatly bless him and would make him into a mighty nation there.

In this new land, Abram moved from place to place since he didn't own any of it. God from time to time reminded Abram of His great promise -- that he would have many descendants who would one day inherit this land. But after many years had passed and Abram and Sarai had become very old, they still had no children. In those days to not be able to bear children was a big disgrace. Since God hadn't yet fulfilled His promise, Abram began to think he would die without an heir and have to leave everything to his head servant.

One day as he was complaining about this to the Lord, God reassured him, once again, that his servant would not be his heir but that he would have a son. God visited Abram one night and took him outside of his tent. God told him to look up at the sky. (Just like Abram, we have to get outside of our circumstances and look up in order to see what God has for us – to

2

take our focus off ourselves and difficulties and get it back on God.)

God pointed out the countless stars to Abram. As Abram gazed up at the multitudes of stars, God made a firm covenant with Abram and gave him, once again, the special promise that he would have a son. He told him that he would someday have so many descendants that they would be as numerous as the stars.

Abram believed God and held onto this covenant promise, but the years continued to roll by without any children. At times, Abram wondered if God's promise would ever come to pass for now both he and his wife were well beyond the child-bearing age.

One day, Sarai, tired of waiting on God, had a bright idea. Why not give her maid servant, Hagar, as a wife to Abram so she could bear children for them. Wow! Now that was brilliant! Not really! However, Abram accepted the idea and Hagar bore him a son, whom they named Ishmael.

Ishmael was born of the flesh and was not the promised son that Sarai and Abram were to have together. Ishmael, born because of unbelief, caused much grief. (How many times do we not fully trust God when He has promised to meet our every need? Any time we act out disobedience or unbelief, we are going to birth "Ishmaels" which will cause us grief and problems. If God doesn't answer our prayers right away, we must stay in faith and wait for His perfect timing. Besides, our problems and importunities are God's opportunities!!!)

When Abram turned 99 and Sarai 90 years old, God appeared to Abram and reminded him to walk blameless before Him. He again reminded Abram of His covenant promise that he would have children without number. In order to help Abram remember this better, God changed his name to Abraham, which means "father of many nations."

Every time someone said his name or Abraham gave his name, he would be reminded of God's promise. God even told Abraham that kings would come from his lineage. God also changed Sarai's name to Sarah, meaning that she would be blessed by being a mother of nations and kings. Finally, God specifically told them that their long promised son would be born the following year.

Sure enough, at the designated time the following year, Sarah bore a son whom she and Abraham named Isaac, just as God had instructed them. Isaac was the blessed son of promise whom they had waited for so long.

Why did it take so many years of waiting for this promise to be fulfilled? Maybe it was because Abraham and Sarah hadn't truly trusted God and their unbelief held it up. Maybe God wanted to prove that nothing is impossible for Him to accomplish. But since God's ways are higher than our ways, we must accept His way of doing things.

As you can imagine, both Sarah and Abraham greatly rejoiced over Isaac. However, their long wait was not wasted for they got to know God better through God's visitations and reminders of the promised son. God had to get them to a place where He could grow their faith and so He could trust them also. Do you have faith in God? Have you earned God's trust? You can do so by loving and obeying Him.

God always wants to give us His best. In order to receive it, we must give Him our all. This sounds scary to some people because they have the mistaken idea that their lives will be miserable if they give themselves wholly to God. After all, He might call them to be a missionary in Africa or make them do something else atrocious. Such nonsense!

If you feel this way about God, you don't realize that as long as you withhold any part of your life, it will result in a life that is unfulfilled, unhappy, and troubled. The most blessed thing you can do is to fully surrender yourself, everyone, and everything which pertains to you to God. Laying down your life to God and entering into His rest is the best thing you can do on this earth, which will not only bless you here but for all eternity. Oh yes, there will be problems and trials, but when you cease from your struggles and fully commit them into God's Hands, God can then work everything out, and you can have joy and victory.

Back to Abraham. God wasn't through with proving Abraham's faith yet for He gave Abraham a really nasty test when Isaac became a young lad. God actually told Abraham to take Isaac, whom he greatly loved, his only promised son, and go to the land of Moriah. There God told Abraham to offer him as a burnt offering. I can't imagine the horrific thoughts which went through Abraham's mind, BUT he had learned to obey God and to trust Him.

The next morning, Abraham got up early, saddled his donkey, split some wood to take along, drug Isaac out of bed, and headed out. To encourage himself, he probably thought about the promises concerning Isaac that God had given him and made himself believe that God would either raise Isaac from the dead or provide another sacrifice.

When you are facing difficulties, it is so important that you stay in faith and proclaim God's promises repeatedly – out loud! God will honor that kind of faith and in turn honor you. As Abraham approached the place of sacrifice, I am sure his heart was beating a hundred times a minute and aching beyond any description.

Isaac asked his father about the situation. "Father, we have the wood and fire, but where is the lamb for the burnt offering?" In faith, Abraham answered, "My son, God will provide for Himself the lamb for the burnt offering." Notice Abraham's answer. This was prophetic of God's own Son, Jesus Christ, laying down His life as a sacrifice for you; for He is the Lamb of God who took your sins so you can stand justified before God and have eternal life.

At this point, when Abraham bound Isaac, Isaac realized that he was to be the sacrificial lamb. By this time, Isaac was a strong boy who could have resisted and gotten free; but he became obedient and submissive to his father, just as Jesus was obedient to His heavenly Father, and allowed Himself to die in your place. I would also imagine that since Abraham was so old, that Isaac probably had to climb onto the altar and lay himself down, just as Jesus willingly laid Himself down on the cruel cross.

As Abraham lifted his hand to kill Isaac with a knife, God stopped him. Abraham had passed the ultimate test of obedience. When Abraham looked behind him, there caught in the bushes, was a ram. The ram (lamb) was sacrificed in place of Isaac. God had provided the lamb for the sacrifice as Abraham had believed. Because Abraham had been willing to obey God and give up his only son, God again blessed Abraham and promised to multiply his descendants as the stars of the heaven and the sand on the seashore.

Your testings and trials are not pleasant either; but if you remain faithful, God will bless you abundantly when you pass your test. There are many ". . . . But God's!" throughout the story of Abraham.

I can do all things through Christ who strengthens me.

Philippians 4:13 NKJV

2. <u>The Smoking Habit Broken</u>

(By Karen Joy King)

As a pastor and Christian Counselor, I have seen many people engulfed in various kinds of bondages and addictions – smoking being one of them. Through the power of God and the spoken word, any kind of bondage can be broken. Below is an example.

Betty (name changed) had tried to quit smoking for many years but couldn't. During that time, she realized she was saying negative things. "I just don't have what it takes." "This is too hard." "I'll never break this addiction." One day a friend recognized what was happening and told Betty to call those things into being which are not (Romans 4:17) and to change her vision and speaking. So she did!

Betty began saying, out loud, by faith, "I don't like to smoke." "I can't stand the taste of nicotine." "When I quit, I'm not going to gain weight." She said those statements every day for several months, even while she was smoking and thoroughly enjoying her cigarettes.

Eventually, the cigarettes began to taste so bad she couldn't stand them any longer. She never smoked again and didn't gain a single ounce. When you speak the right words, God goes to work for you, not by your own strength but in His ". . . <u>But God!</u>"

I was sought by those who did not ask for Me:

I was found by those who did not seek Me.

Isaiah 65:1 NKJV

3. Jesus Wouldn't Let Go

(By Karen Joy King)

God certainly works in mysterious ways! Why it is that He seems to try harder to bring some people to Him than others? Maybe one reason might be that someone is praying for them. The example of the man below shows how patient and merciful God is for God could have let him continue in his sin and be lost for all eternity. The moral of this story is – don't fight God. Just yield in the first place and be happier much sooner.

For years, a Christian wife was married to a man who didn't want anything to do with Christ, let alone watch TV ministers. For years, the wife had prayed for him and tried to get him to watch Christian broadcasting on TV since she couldn't get him to go to church with her. But this man vehemently refused. However, one day as he was flipping TV channels he landed on a Christian program. The preaching was convicting, so he quickly tried to change channels, but the remote no longer worked.

No matter what he did, including changing the batteries, it wouldn't work. He tried not to listen ". . . But God!" was at work in his life. Through that incident, the man's life was changed. He accepted Christ as his Savior and now regularly attends church with his wife. The strange thing was that as soon as the TV program was over, the remote worked perfectly ". . . But God!"

And my God shall supply all your need
according to His riches in glory.
Philippians 4:19 NKJV

4. Poor Boy Gets Shoes

(By Karen Joy King)

I heard this story a long time ago, and it has meant a lot to me, so I want to share it here.

Many years ago, there was a young lad who lived in an inner city. His parents were very poor and all he had known throughout his young life were sad-looking, ill-fitting hand-me-down clothes.

When the weather had turned cold, the poor little guy had no shoes or socks. After school one day, he stood in front of a store window dreamily gazing at a new pair of shoes. Along came a lady who stopped and asked him why he was staring into the window. He told her that he was praying for God to give him a pair of shoes.

The lady's heart melted almost to tears, so she gently took him by the hand and led him into the store. There she asked for some water and soap and proceeded to wash the boy's dirty, cold feet. She bought him several pairs of socks and put one pair on

17

his feet. Then she told him to pick out a nice pair of shoes, which he did.

While the lady was paying for the shoes and socks; the boy, with tears running down his cheeks, looked up into the kind lady's face and asked, "Are you God's wife?" God had seen this precious boy's need, had intervened, and had provided for him through this gracious lady ". . . <u>But God!</u>" The boy saw her as a part of God.

Are you on the lookout for others who have needs? You, too, when you intervene and help others, become a part of God.

Burdens are lifted at Calvary.
Jesus is very near.
John Moore

5. <u>God Lifted My Burden</u>

(By Karen Joy King)

Having moved many times, I bought a house in which I thought I would remain until I departed for heaven. However, God had other plans. After my dad died, I took care of my elderly mother and the family farm.

As Mom's health continued to fail, along with her eyesight, I had to make more and more trips to the farm to care for her, which was a 24 mile round trip. Also, in order to do this, I had to take a minimum wage job in order to have flexible hours for these trips.

Besides my trips, others who had volunteered their time along with some hired help, it was not enough. Mom needed someone to be with her all the time. In the back of my mind, I knew that God wanted me to sell my house and move in with her.

However, <u>I didn't want to sell and move again</u>, so I battled this for over a year. Finally, I obeyed God and sold my house. Even though I knew this was God's will, my heart was heavy. As I drove away from my house for the last time, I prayed, "Father, take away every desire I have for this house and never let me miss it." He did ". . . <u>But God</u>!"

As one whom his mother comforts

So will I comfort you;

And you shall be comforted

Isaiah 66:13 NKJV

6. **God Lifted Another Burden**

(By Karen Joy King)

In the previous story, I shared about moving in with my mom to take care of her and the family farm where she still lived after my dad died. I was able to care for her several years until she needed 24/7 care at which time, I had to put her in a nursing home. That was very difficult for me to do, and I cried for a long time.

I remained at the farm and cared for it several more years until Mom died December 28, 2005. To say the least, it was a very difficult Christmas!

Since neither of my brothers wanted the farm and it was too much for me to keep, we sold it. This was another very difficult time for me since I had been born and raised on this lovely farm. I had some very deep roots and precious memories there; plus it had been in the family for over 130 years. It was heart breaking for me to give it up, especially since it was sold to someone outside the family.

Once again, as I was driving away for the last time, I asked God to remove all feelings for the place so I would not miss it and grieve over having to give it up. He did ". . . <u>But God</u>! In its place, He gave me a wonderful home about three miles away.

The He (Jesus) arose and rebuked the wind,
and said to the sea, Peace, be still!"
And the wind ceased and there
was a great calm.

Mark 4:39 NKJV

7. Jesus Stills the Storm

(Paraphrased from Matthew 8:23-27)

(By Karen Joy King)

One of my favorite incidents in the New Testament (actually I have many) is recorded in the Gospels. I will take the version from Matthew 8: 23-27. "When He (Jesus) got into the boat, His disciples followed Him. And behold, there arose a great storm on the sea, so that the boat was being covered with the waves; but Jesus Himself was asleep. And they came to Him and woke Him, saying, 'Save us, Lord; we are perishing!' He said to them, 'Why are you afraid, you men of little faith?'"

"Then He got up and rebuked the winds and the sea, and it became perfectly calm. The men were amazed, and said, 'What kind of a man is this, that even the winds and the sea obey Him?'" "… But God!"

Are you in some kind of storm? Just call upon Jesus and let Him calm your storm. The important thing to remember is that you can be in the storm, but don't let the storm get in you.

The Lord shall preserve you from all evil.

Psalm 121:7 NKJV

8. Stubborn Table – Thank God It Was Stubborn!

(By Karen Joy King)

Tragedies are God's opportunities for impossibilities. God is the Giver of all good things! When you are in the midst of bad things, take some time, write down all good things you have, and then thank God for them. Then when you become discouraged, read through your list and be reminded of how God has been at work in your life. He is always bigger than any problem you can face. He doesn't want you to struggle with any problem, but to commit yourself and your circumstance to Him so He can work on your behalf.

It is important to remember that your faith won't always instantly deliver you out of every problem, but it can carry you through them. God uses difficult circumstances to develop you so you can be ready to receive greater things from Him. Sometimes the thing you are praying for isn't God's best for you; so if He doesn't answer your prayer in the way you think, it may not be the best timing or the best for you, or maybe He is protecting you from a danger. Instead of getting all upset and impatient, simply learn to rest in Him and affirm that you are trusting Him to work in your behalf.

There was once a preacher traveling on a small jet and wanted to pull the table out to do some work. It was fastened to the side of the plane instead of the back of the seat ahead, which he thought was strange. He yanked, pulled, and tried everything to get it open, but nothing worked. He prayed for God to help him and under his breath, he remarked, "I'm going to get this open if this is the last thing I ever do."

About that time one of the men across the aisle saw his struggles and came over to see if he could assist the preacher, but all his efforts were futile, too. Finally, the preacher moved to another seat, and it was then he saw he had been sitting by an emergency exit door. Had God answered his prayer, it would have been the last thing he would have ever done ". . . But God!" God had protected him from his own prayer! It is truly best to trust God in all circumstances!

So, if you don't immediately receive an answer to prayer, take time to seek God and find out what His will for you is during your difficulty. His plans for you are always good – always! By being patient and learning to wait upon Him, you will get to know Him better. Knowing God is the best thing you can accomplish in this lifetime and for all eternity; even better than getting some prayers answered.

In the Appendix, I have outlined a way to better develop your spiritual eyes and ears. God is always speaking to you and wanting to show you His will, but you won't hear or see Him unless you are correctly postured, listening, looking, and expecting.

God's ways are higher that your ways. What may seem unfathomable, non-understandable, and tragic to you, God is somehow using it for your good. He doesn't waste anything. However, you may never fully understand it until you are with Him in heaven.

Take for instance the horrendous tragedy in Horatio G. Spafford's life. He was a wealthy lawyer and business man in the 1800's. When his wife and four daughters were crossing the Atlantic Ocean, their vessel collided with another ship, and Spafford lost all four of his daughters.

After he received word from his wife about this tragedy, he booked a passage across the Atlantic to be with her. As the ship crossed the spot where the horrible accident had taken place, the captain pointed it out to Spafford. Spafford's heart was greatly grieved as he stared solemnly at the spot; but later that night, he wrote the famous hymn *It is Well With My Soul.*

This beloved hymn has blessed many over the years and its words have provided comfort to others during their unfortunate circumstances. So no matter what your circumstance, you need to turn it all over into God's hands, remain at rest and peace in Him, and learn to say, "It is well with my soul."

"When sorrows like sea billows roll, whatever my lot, You (God) have taught me to say, 'It is well, it is well with my soul.'" Yes, life has a way of throwing curves at us and many times when least expected; but remember, when you are trusting and resting in God, it will be well with you, even through sorrow and loss. Learn to say, "Maybe things aren't as I would like them; but I am trusting, You, God, knowing that You are in control and all will be well."

Behold what manner of love the Father has
bestowed on us, that we should be called
children of God!

I John 3:1 NKJV

9. The First Time I Saw God Smile at Me

(By Karen Joy King)

At the time, I was a young Christian and trying to do everything God wanted me to do. Having quiet times with God was top priority throughout the day and many times during the night. One of those times was every night just before I climbed into bed, I would kneel by my bed, pray, and meditate on some scriptures.

One night, I was very tired and didn't spend much time praying and meditating. As a result, when I climbed into bed, I was feeling guilty over my short session with God. Once in bed and nicely tucked under my covers, I suddenly became aware of Jesus above me and smiling at me.

This was the first time I had ever encountered anything like this, but certainly not the last. His smile reassured me that in His sight, I was well-beloved and didn't need to feel guilty ". . . But God!"

God never makes you feel guilty. That is satan's business. So if you feel guilty, focus on God and let Him smile at you. Since that initial time, I have experienced God's smile many times! Sometimes when I am working at my computer or doing other things, I will be suddenly stopped by the sense that Jesus is smiling at me, reminding me of His great love for me! God wants you to be able to see and hear Him for He is your constant, loving Companion. (See the Appendix to learn how to see God.)

My God sent His angel

Daniel 6:22a NKJV

10. An Angel Drove My Car

(By Karen Joy King)

One night I was driving a friend and her three children from Jackson, Michigan, to my home in Pioneer, Ohio. A semi was coming from the opposite direction when suddenly a pickup truck started to pass it.

I was about to have a head on crash with the pick-up when an angel took control of my steering wheel and steered my car onto the shoulder (fortunately, at that particular spot in the highway, there was a wide shoulder) just in the nick of time. All three vehicles passed safely on a two-lane highway. After passing, the angel gently steered my car back into my lane ". . . But God!"

Ordinarily, I would have been so shook up that I wouldn't have known what to do, but I felt very calm and thanked God for His protection! This is a reminder that God's children have ministering angels assigned to them. That night certainly proved that to me!

An Angel
Drawn by Heidi Smith

The angel of the Lord encamps
all around those who fear (reverence) Him,
and delivers them.

Psalm 34:7 NKJV

11. <u>Another Angel Incident</u>

(By Karen Joy King)

It was very late at night another time when I was driving home from Jackson, Michigan, to my home in Pioneer, Ohio. Usually, I don't get sleepy at the wheel. I was about a mile from Pioneer when all of a sudden, someone slapped my hand. I heard it and felt it, but there was no one in the car with me.

I had fallen asleep, but that slap saved me from wrecking my car and possible injuries. Once again, my angel came to my assistance and protected me. The slap came as I was crossing the yellow line and woke me up in time to safely guide my car back into my lane ". . . <u>But God</u>!"

He/She shall call upon Me, and I will answer
him/her; I will be with him/her in trouble;
I will deliver him/her.

Psalm 91:15 NKJV

12. <u>Desperate at Gas Station</u>

(By Karen Joy King)

Has God ever asked you to do something quite out of the ordinary which could be very embarrassing? One day, a man (let's call him Bob) drove into a gas station to fill up his car and to pick up some food. While there, he had the strongest impression that he should go into the restroom and stand on his head.

At that point, Bob thought he was losing his mind. Ignoring it, he left the building and got into his car, but the impression became stronger. He sat in his car for a while trying to figure out what to do. As he did, he became even more impressed he should do this seemingly ridiculous thing. Finally, he said, "All right, God, if this is what You want me to do, so be it. I will be a fool for You."

Bob went into the restroom and stood on his head; but don't you know, another man (let's call him Tim) came in. Bob felt very foolish when all of a sudden Tim began to sob. Bob asked him, "What is the matter?"

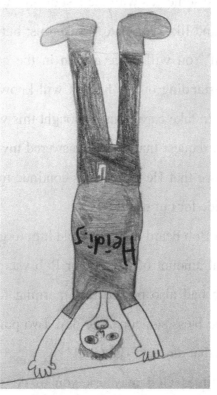

Man Standing on Head
Drawn by Heidi Smith

Tim, between sobs answered, "I have been out of a job for a long time. My family has no money with which to buy food or to pay our rent. On the way here, to purchase some gas with the last of my money, I felt hopeless and like God had forsaken us; but I prayed, "Father, if You will place a man in the gas station restroom standing on his head, I will know that You are going to take care of us. I thought this was such a ridiculous request that if God answered my prayer, it would prove that He really does continue to care and will provide for our needs."

When Bob heard that, God told him to give Tim a substantial amount of money, for Bob was a wealthy man. Bob had also prayed that morning for God to use him to bless someone that day. Two prayers were answered that day ". . . <u>But God</u>!"

Sometimes God may ask you to do something uncomfortable in order to help others. If He does, give yourself time to prove it is God and then do it! Not everything God does is about you.

Many are the afflictions of the righteous, But
the Lord delivers him/her out of them all.
Psalm 34:19 NKJV

13. <u>Don't Waste Your Pain</u>

(By Karen Joy King)

When I was much younger and hadn't been married for too many years; and after I had my first baby, a very dear friend of mine moved to another state, due to her husband's work, quite far from me, which was devastating to both of us. Here's the story.

During my pregnancy, she had lovingly and faithfully taken care of me since I had been very ill and too sick to care for myself. Each morning when my husband left for work, he dropped me off at my friend's house.

Each morning she would welcome me with a big smile and loving friendship. Every day she poured her life into me and nurtured me. She would make sure I rested comfortably, brought me my meals, and helped me to the restroom. She also dropped her work and spent time talking with me so I wouldn't be alone. This went on for almost my whole pregnancy. Not once did she ever complain about this responsibility she so graciously had taken on.

After work, my husband would pick me up and take me home. Often this kind lady sent food home with us for our evening meal.

When she and her husband decided to move south, I was devastated and wondered how I would get along without her, for even after I had my baby, we remained very close friends.

They made several trips to their new home before actually moving there permanently. The last time I saw her drive down the road, I crumbled with the biggest broken heart I'd ever had. As I was watching her departure out my bedroom window which faced the road, I fell down beside my bed and cried until I couldn't cry any more. I told the Lord that I couldn't stand this and had to have His help to face the days ahead without my best friend. Instantly, He took my broken heart away, lifted my unbearable burden, and put a peace and calm there instead. I was able at that instant to rise and look at life with a renewed joy and purpose ". . . <u>But God</u>!"

There was no way I could have manufactured such peace when my heart had been so broken and devastated. But that is my wonderful, personal God Who cares about all of us in every situation at all times. All you have to do is to call upon Him and He will answer you during your time of heartbreak. "Call upon Me, and I will answer you, and show you great and mighty things which you do not know." (Jeremiah 33:3) Had I just fallen down by my bed without calling upon Him, I would not have received His help. This time, His help was instantaneous.

But what if God had chosen not to immediately answer my prayer and left me with what seemed like an unbearable burden? God's ways are always perfect. His timing is always perfect. He is perfect and knows the end from the beginning.

Sometimes, He allows us to go through a trial in order to strength us and develop our character. In that case, He gives us the grace, strength, joy, and peace we need. However, the sooner we submit to Him, give Him our circumstances, and begin to trust and rejoice in Him, the sooner He will bring us through the situation.

If we start complaining and wrongfully accuse God about our circumstance, the longer it will last. Remember the Israelites when they had come out of Egypt after being slaves for four hundred years? They complained over and over, and God instantly killed many of them on the spot.

I don't think complaining goes over very well with God; in fact, I know it doesn't. But He loves it when during the trial, we offer the sacrifice of praise. This shows we are trusting Him and believing that He will work everything out for our good. AND the trial will be over before you know it, plus you will be a stronger, better person for it.

You might say, "Well, I have asked God for help but I didn't receive anything." He may have given you more help than you may have realized at that moment. Just because God doesn't answer your prayer with the immediate deliverance you think you need and should have, does not mean God hasn't heard you. He is always working to make you and your circumstances better. If your answer is delayed, maybe it wasn't His timing, maybe He is waiting so He can give you something better, or maybe He is protecting you.

When you are intent upon seeking God's hand instead of His face, in other words, enjoying His gifts instead of the Giver, sometimes in order to help you find the abundant life He has promised you, He disrupts your life so that you release your grasp of your present life. Usually through pain or loss, God asks you to let go of the things you love so He can give you more. The first thing He wants is for you to fully give your heart to Him.

When you are trying to make life work for yourself, He hinders the process by causing your efforts to fail so you realize that you can do nothing in your own strength or without Him. (John 15:5) If you truly don't know God, usually when something doesn't work out, anger towards God is the normal reaction. I know, for I used to throw my fist into the air at God in a rage and sometimes threw my Bible across the room and then go stomp on it. But, thank God, I don't act that way anymore.

I used to ask, "Why doesn't God help me?" "Why can't I find victory and live the abundant life He has promised?" I should have asked the following questions, "Why aren't I more fully given to God and in love with Him?" "Where is my focus? On God and His power or on myself and my problem?" "Father, what is Your will for me?"

God shouldn't be a means to your end but the Way Himself. (John 14:6) If you make God to be your assistant instead of God as your life, you will be defeated and disappointed. In order to have the abundant life He has promised, you must come to the place where you are fully His and He is your all. If you are not in that place, then you will be surprised and overtaken by life's events.

God does want you to be happy, but He knows that until you are holy like Him, you cannot really be happy. "Until God has become our all, and we are fully his, we will continue to make idols of the good things He gives us." *p. 87 -- Walking With God by John Eldredge*

Deuteronomy 13:3, "The Lord your God is testing you to find out whether you love him with all your heart and with all your soul." Through God's testing, He thwarts your efforts to bring yourself to Him. It is only through the Father that you can come to Jesus Christ. (John 6:44)

Please keep in mind that God doesn't cause the pain in your life. Pain comes when you disobey God and through satanic attacks. "Many are the afflictions of the righteous, but God delivers them out of them all." (Ps. 34:19) Since pain does come, what are you going to do with it? Ask God to show you what He wants you to understand and how He wants to redeem you through it. Don't waste your pain!

Before I formed you in the womb, I knew you,
And before you were born I consecrated you.

Jeremiah 1:5 NKJV

14. <u>My Journey With God</u>

(By Karen Joy King)

My journey with God began before I was born. "Before I formed you in the womb, I knew you, and before you were born I consecrated you." (Jeremiah 1:5) My mother had two boys before me. The younger one drowned when he was about four years old before I was born. She wanted a girl and a child who would be a musician. So she prayed. God answered her prayer and gave her me ". . . <u>But God</u>!"

From as far back as I can remember, I had a fascination and love for music. I would rather go to a music store than a toy store. I loved watching band and choir directors. I loved listening to music and wanted to learn how to play many instruments!

During my oldest brother's band concert, when I was around two years old, I stood on my chair and tried to mimic the band director. This caught the attention of the whole auditorium of listeners. They laughed and thought I was pretty cute!

54

When I was a few years older, I begged to take piano lessons; because at that time, I was fascinated with the famous pianist Liberace. I loved the flash of his rings and sparkly coat, which he would make a show of flipping its tails before sitting on the piano bench. His big fancy candelabra also caught my eye! Then when he started playing, I thought there couldn't be anything that sounded so beautiful! I wanted to play the piano like Liberace!

Mom found a piano teacher, and I was excited. Being very young and <u>very</u> naïve, I thought I was going to be able to take one lesson and come home playing like Liberace. Imagine my disgust and disappointment when all I learned to play at my first lesson were a couple of whole notes! However, that was the beginning of my musical training.

Throughout the following years, I was able to learn to play many instruments and earned a Bachelor of Arts degree with an applied major in music! I officially became a music teacher and director in several schools and churches. I say "officially" because I had actually taught music long before earning my degree!

This is an example of a ". . . <u>But God</u>!" for my mom. Mom had prayed, and God gave her the desires of her heart. "Delight yourself also in the Lord; and He shall give you the desires of your heart." (Psalm 37:4)

Many times people fail to see the ". . . <u>But God</u>" in their lives and call it mere luck or that it just the way it happened. Throughout this book, I hope to awaken your realization of God at work in your life and all around you. He is a God Who is interested in you before you were born and loves you with an everlasting and unconditional love.

But you may be thinking, "Well, no one prayed for me to be born; in fact, I wasn't even wanted. I have been abused all my life, and certainly don't see God in any of my life or surroundings."

Believe me, my home while growing up and while married were far from perfect, too. We can't choose the parents we have nor the home in which we grow up; but as we mature, we become responsible for the choices we make, for what we believe, and how we speak and act.

No one's life is perfect, but we can choose to live it well, break out of the bondages that hold us, learn to see God and allow Him to bless us. When you choose to live life as God instructs you to do, then you can have ". . . <u>But God</u>" incidents in your life, too. Actually, you already have. You just need to recognize them.

If you don't immediately receive an answer to prayer or your pleas for help, take time to seek God and find out what His will for you is during your difficulty. His plans for you are always good; and by waiting upon Him, you will get to know Him better. Knowing God is the best thing you can accomplish in this life time and for all eternity.

In the Appendix, I have outlined a way to develop your spiritual eyes and ears. God is always speaking and revealing His will, but you won't hear or see Him unless you are correctly postured, listening, and looking.

Delight yourself also in the Lord, and He shall give you the desires of your heart.

Psalm 37:4 NKJV

15. <u>The Little White Bible</u>

(By Karen Joy King)

Since I was valedictorian of my high school graduating class, I wanted to go to college and make a good career for myself. My family was rather poor, so my dad gave me enough money to pay for one semester. Before I completed that semester, I began to look for work so I could continue. After checking several job openings, I found one and thought I could pay for another semester, but from having studied so hard for so many years, I was burned out. Besides that, I was very homesick. At the end of the first semester, I moved back home.

During my first and only semester at Olivet Nazarene University, I came across some students who held some dynamic prayer meetings. Even though I had attended church all my life, I thirsted for a much deeper and meaningful spiritual walk. These students seemed to have those experiences for which I hungered.

They were "on fire for God" and would often go out on street corners, into the highways and the byways, and witness, then they would come back to the prayer meetings and share about those they had won to Christ. Those were some blessed times of fellowship and worship for me.

Having tasted this spiritual life, when I came home, I wanted to find a church "on fire for God." As a child, my family had sometimes attended special music services at a very conservative church because we knew the pastor since he had given my oldest brother piano lessons. We really enjoyed the musical programs there.

Upon returning home from the university, I stayed home a few Sundays and listened to church services on my radio. Remembering the "on fire" services at Olivet, I decided to try the musical, conservative church because I had felt God's presence there while enjoying the musical services.

My youngest brother was also hungering for a closer relationship with God, so he went with me to this church. At first, we sat on the back pew laughing at the

people when they became so excited about the Lord—
we just weren't used to this kind of exuberance during
church services even though I wanted some "fire" in
the services. It wasn't long, though, until God drew us
in and we became exuberant, too!

Soon, our mother began to come with us. What a
time we had in the Lord at that church. God's presence
was so real during each service. We not only met on
Sunday mornings, but on Sunday nights and various
nights through the week.

Sometimes on Sunday afternoons, we would meet
to have music practice and then go minister at jails
and nursing homes. Many times on Tuesday nights, we
would have another music practice. Thursday nights
were prayer meeting nights. Sometimes on Friday
nights, we'd have prayer and fast meetings. The youth
had their meetings on Saturday nights. We loved all this
activity and couldn't wait until the next service!

Anytime we attended the church, we were so
blessed and empowered by the Holy Spirit that we didn't
want to leave. Sometimes on Sunday nights after the

service had ended, a group of us would stay around the altar praying and rejoicing until midnight or later. Reluctantly, we left because we either had to go school or work the next morning.

During many of the services, the Holy Spirit would break in upon us and the whole order would be changed. We were free to worship as God directed us. If God laid a song or chorus on someone's heart, they would burst out singing with the whole congregation joining in.

Maybe someone would have a burning testimony on their heart, so the pastor would let them testify in the middle of his sermon. Many sermons were never preached because God took over. During these times, people would get saved, some healed, or some slain in the Spirit—we just had great times in the Lord.

When the congregation sang the choruses and hymns, often times going from one to another spontaneously, (fortunately, our musicians were able to play both by note and by ear, so they had no problem keeping up with the singing); it seemed like heaven and earth met. God's glorious presence filled the sanctuary and our hearts! It was so wonderful it is almost impossible to describe.

During my time at that church, my car needed some mechanical work done. I was just a teenager at the time and a little on the shy order. An excellent mechanic lived in my community, so I decided to drive by his house on the way home from work one day and set up an appointment. When I parked in front of his house and was ready to get out of my car, I felt God prompting me to take my white Bible with me to the door. It was laying on the car seat beside me.

All kinds of thoughts entered my head as to why it would be totally silly and embarrassing to take the Bible to the door when all I wanted to do was to set up an appointment to get my car fixed. Each time I started to open the car door to get out, I was pulled back and felt an overwhelming need to take that Bible with me. Again and again, I tried to talk myself out of this, but at last I knew I had to obey God and take my Bible to the door with me.

As I approached the porch to knock on the house door, I still felt very embarrassed and awkward. When the mechanic's wife opened the door, I laid the Bible on the porch railing, but she saw me. Her first words were, "Oh, don't lay it there, it might get dirty." I replied that it was ok and asked to set up an appointment with her mechanic husband.

All the while we were talking, she kept eyeing my Bible. As soon as I had made my appointment, she began to tell me about her life, that she was very depressed, and was planning to take her life that night. I asked her if I could come back that evening and talk with her further since I had another appointment I needed to go to. She agreed to talk with me and to not do anything drastic ". . . . But God!"

Now what if I hadn't obeyed God's prompting and had refused to take my Bible with me to the door? Things would have turned out much differently. This lady would have taken her life.

Later that evening, I picked her up and we talked as I drove out to a spot in the country where we could have the privacy since her husband was now home for the evening. She shared that their marriage wasn't going well plus a lot of other things that were really bothering her.

Since she wasn't a Christian, she didn't know how to turn her burdens over to God and let Him work. After talking and praying with her, she felt better and promised me that she wouldn't commit suicide. She also promised to go to church with me the following Sunday.

She kept her word and continued to go to church with me week after week. Upon hearing the salvation message of the Gospel, she repented of her sins and asked Jesus Christ to come into her life as her Savior. What a glorious change ". . . <u>But God!</u>" Her life was transformed instantly; and instead of having the worried, depressed facial look, her face glowed! She had become a new creature in Christ and she was full of joy! (2 Corinthians 5:17)

Her marriage improved! A few years after her conversion, her husband became very ill and was taken to the hospital. On his death bed, with the guidance and prayers of our pastors, this man gave his life to Jesus Christ and went home to be with his new-found Savior ". . . <u>But God</u>!"

This lady became a pianist in our church, led others in her family to Christ, and was a powerful witness for Christ in her community of Fayette, Ohio. This story would not have turned out like this if God wouldn't have intervened in this woman's life by having me take my Bible to her door ". . . <u>But God</u>!"

Oh how He loves each one of us! Maybe He hasn't instructed someone to carry a Bible to your door, but if you call out to Him, He will guide you to people who care and to Himself, the One Who died for you so you can have abundant life and an eternity with Him!

You can trust the One Who died for you! He has a life so much better for you if you will accept Him. If you pray the following prayer from your heart, God will accept you into His family and kingdom! He will bless you beyond your wildest imagination!

"Dear Jesus, I recognize my need of You. My life hasn't been going so well. Please forgive me of all my sins and come into my life as my Savior. Take my life and make it all You want it to be, and help me to obey you in everything You ask me to do. Thank You for dying for me! Amen."

Begin reading your Bible. A good place to start is the Gospel of John in the New Testament. Find a good church wherein you can fellowship with other believers, hear the pure Word of God preached, and grow in your new-found faith.

But if you don't forgive,
neither will your Father in heaven
forgive your trespasses.

Mark 11:26 NKJV

16. <u>Will You Forgive Him?</u>

(From Sue)

Several years ago in November of 2007, I was coming home from an evening appointment with a client. Around 9:00 P.M. I pulled into my garage. Even though I didn't see anyone, just as I was stepping out of my car there was a 17ish year old, Hispanic young man standing behind my daughter's car. He said to me, "I need a ride."

I'm usually not the type to think poorly or negatively of individuals; for many times I have left my purse in a store cart and walk two aisles away not thinking for a minute that someone would actually steal it. I prefer to think of the best of people, BUT in that moment when I saw that young man's eyes, I saw evil. I don't believe I have ever heard God's audible voice up to that point; but that night in my garage **I KNOW** I heard the Lord's voice, and **I KNOW** I heard Him say, "Get back in your car!" I just knew that young man did not have good intentions!

As I tried to swing my legs back in the car, he had already rushed the door and had begun trying to pull the door open and pull me out. As he was trying to pry the door open, I was desperately trying to get it closed; but my leg was still in the opening, and he was much stronger than me.

Once he was able to open the door, he continued to pull me from the car. Since the space was narrow, he became enraged when he couldn't get me out. That's when he began to pummel my face. I was pinned in, so I couldn't protect myself.

At one point, he hit me so hard that his blow not only crushed my glasses into my face but also knocked me sideways into the passenger seat. This gave me an advantage since I was now level and could kick him while screaming "rape" and "fire". (I had learned never to yell "help"). I couldn't honk the horn since he knocked my keys from my hand during one of his punches.

Funny side note – just that day I had gone to the dentist and been given a toothbrush which I had placed in my center console. While being punched and pulled, I remembered the toothbrush, so I reached in and attempted to grab the toothbrush. I figured it would be something with which to defend myself.

I grabbed a long skinny object and whipped it up towards his face, but instead of the toothbrush, it was a tampon. Maybe that's what scared him – maybe he thought I was going to do something that I shouldn't with that thing!

Being either frustrated or frightened, he finally fled. When I felt he was gone, I went into my house while calling the police on my cell and calling to my family for help. The chaos that ensued after that is really crazy.

Later that evening, the police asked me to go with them to see if I could identify a 'suspect' who had just been picked up around the corner for the same type of crime and who fit the description I had given to them. The only difference was that he had stabbed that individual while attempting to take his car. **Sure enough, it was the kid who had attacked me.**

During the following weeks, I began to develop prejudice, bitterness, and most notably, fear. I was afraid to come home in the dark. I was afraid of sleeping. I was afraid of men being in my 'space'. I was afraid when people approached me somewhat quickly. I had just become afraid of everything.

Several months after the attempted carjacking, I had a full-circle, defining moment as a result of an incident on the way to church one day. I stopped to get a cup of coffee and there was a young man, about 16 or 17 years old, standing on the sidewalk asking for money. After getting what I needed, I got back into my car. I saw that young man standing there and it made me think of a friend's son who lived on the streets with a drug problem.

I got back out of my car and asked him if he was hungry. When he said he was, I took him inside the eatery and bought him a sandwich, chips, and soda. I paid for it and got back into my car.

As I looked in my rear view mirror, I saw the boy coming towards me. My heart began to race so fast I couldn't breathe. I couldn't seem to find the buttons quickly enough to get my window closed; but when he was at my window, I must have looked like **a psycho chick,** but with tears in his eyes he only said, "That was a kind thing you did."

By the look on my face and the panic in my eyes, that boy must have thought that I was afraid of him because he was black. Although his race had nothing to do with it, it had everything to do with him being a male who could harm me....again, and that bothered me even more.

When he left, I wept. And then I became raging mad due to the anger that had been building up in me for some time. With each passing day, I became even more angry. I was so angry at the young man who had hurt me because I was now living in a state of fear, cynicism, and prejudice. I couldn't sleep because the young attacker had taken away my security.

I was now engulfed with unforgiveness and it was turning me into someone I didn't like. I already had enough issues, but now I was becoming angry with issues! BUT -- I knew what needed to be done to get over my anger -- I needed to forgive my attacker! **But could I really forgive him and give him that satisfaction?! God always finds a way to drive home a point.**

One morning, I was standing in my bathroom putting on my makeup, when all of a sudden, the mirror became a movie screen of a court room. In it I saw the defense team on the right, the prosecuting team on the left, and the judge in the front.

I heard the question, "What are the charges?" The list was read – seven felony counts with each one listed one by one: two counts assault, two counts attempted carjacking, terrorist threat, battery, etc... I heard the judge ask the question, "How do you plead?" The response was, "Not guilty."

The whole scene in my mirror seemed to fast-forward and suddenly the trial appeared to be ending. The judge asked us all to rise since he was ready to pronounce his verdict. The judge again listed the charges, and one by one the young man (my attacker) was found guilty on all counts. The judge gave him the sentence of 40 years in prison.

I remember thinking, "That's kinda long." My guess was that he needed drug counseling; and yes, he needed to be punished (and I wanted him to be punished); but 40 years seemed kind of stiff and that saddened me because he was only 17 years old. Make no mistake, I wanted him to be punished because I was madder than a hornet; but for a moment, I imagined him as someone's child being put away for so long. Being a mom myself, it touched my heart.

I heard the judge ask if there was anything else before the case is closed. In my mirror vision, I saw myself standing before THE Judge (God). Although, I couldn't see His face, I felt His presence. I asked Him if the sentence could be changed....a little. His response was a firm, "NO!" With a booming voice, I heard him say, "Justice mandates that someone must pay the penalty for the crime and the punishment, and for these crimes, it's 40yrs. The ONLY alternative is that someone else must pay the penalty, but the penalty must be paid. That's what justice is."

In a flash, I heard myself say, "I'll take the punishment." Without hesitation, THE Judge admonished me, "You will be treated like a criminal and will have no rights. All his guilt will fall on you, and you will not be able to murmur or complain. You will have no voice for you are willingly taking his guilt on yourself, and he will be free. Do you understand?" I just nodded my head.

Instantly, I saw myself walking down a corridor of a correctional facility and was holding what appeared to be clothes, blankets, etc. I was mortified as I heard the jeers, comments, and saw them grabbing for me. I saw myself in a room where they were strip-searching me, and I remember feeling mortified. I never felt so humiliated, but the Lord allowed me to experience every single sense of imprisonment, even the smell.

During this entire time, I knew I was innocent but couldn't say a word for I had willingly taken his punishment. I had given up my rights to defend myself.

It was simply the worst feeling in the world being completely innocent, yet being treated so unfairly.

Suddenly I found myself back in the courtroom standing before THE Judge. This time THE Judge had a face and it was the Lord's. His words were simple yet firm, and they just about killed me. He said, "Just as I have forgiven you for all that you are guilty of, I am **asking** you to forgive your attacker. Will you forgive him?"

In a moment, all the lessons on forgiveness came to mind with ONE very real awareness -- **forgiveness is a choice**. **The Lord asked me to forgive him.** Although the Bible mandates it, **He had asked me**. He knew that my **healing could not begin until I chose to forgive.** I was given a first-hand revelation behind the passage 'pray for your enemies, **SO THAT YOU may be healed**'. (Colossians 3:13) When you pray for your enemies, your heart can't hold on to un-forgiveness. My healing didn't happen overnight, but in time it did happen ". . . <u>But God!</u>"

If you can believe,

all things are possible to him/her who

believes."

Mark 9:23 NKJV

17. <u>I Completed 10 University Courses in Less Than 3 Months</u>

(From Avanell)

It was the end of August, and I would soon have been unemployed for two years. The severance package I had received from my former employer contained funds to be used for retraining, but the eligibility requirements stated that the courses I took would need to be completed within two years of my termination date.

I had felt the Lord prompting me to take counseling courses eight months before, but I had been concerned about being able to get the extra funding so I had laid it aside. And here He was, prompting me once again, drawing me to Christian Leadership University.

With the second prompting, I decided that God really did want me to do this. So, if He had truly called me to do this, then He would enable me to complete the ten courses for a Counseling Certificate within the allotted time frame. By the time I decided to enroll, I now only had four months in which to complete ten courses.

When I talked with the admissions person at CLU, she said it would probably take at least six months to complete ten courses and that it was pretty much "humanly impossible" to do it in the amount of time I had to meet the eligibility requirements.

"For with God nothing will be impossible." Luke 2:37, has always been one of my favorite verses of Scripture. And another one is Mark 9:23; "Jesus said to him, 'If you can believe, all things are possible to him who believes.'" This challenge to meet my eligibility requirements was simply another opportunity for God to show Himself strong on my behalf.

By the time I got enrolled, received my funding, and obtained the course material it was September 21, 2010, and I needed to have the ten courses done by February 1, 2011. Dr. Karen Joy King, my instructor at CLU, said this was a very short time frame in which to complete this many courses but she would do her best to help me reach my goal.

She helped me set goals for course completion dates, and as I worked diligently to attain those goals, the Lord supernaturally infused me with His wisdom, understanding and power to complete all course requirements on or before the goal dates. With Dr. King's help, prayers from my friends and family, and help from my husband in studying for my tests, I was able to reach my goal on January 21, 2011, a full ten days ahead of schedule! Ten courses in less than three months -- the impossible goal met ". . . <u>But God!</u>"

Through all of this, I learned that if I seek God with my whole heart, He will help me rise up to the challenges and attain the goals of whatever He has called me to do. For with God nothing will be impossible ". . .<u>But God!</u>"

The Graduate with Degree
Drawn by Heidi Smith

For the Lord God is a sun and shield;

The Lord will give grace and glory;

No good thing will He withhold from those

who walk uprightly.

Psalm 84:11 NKJV

18. <u>My Gift From God</u>

(From Avanell)

In September 2007 after a 7 1/2 week marriage, I suddenly found myself a widow. I was devastated and felt that life was over. I had been on a new job for only four months, was living in a large city, and only had a few friends from church and work. I entered the darkest period of my life. I had to force myself to get out of bed each morning. It was only through a willful effort that I was able to go to work, to church, to pray and read my Bible.

My superiors at work helped me through this time by having people check my work to make sure I wasn't making costly errors. My Life Group at church constantly checked on me and encouraged me to go on. My family kept in touch with me to make sure I was doing okay, and close friends from where I had formerly lived spent time with me on the phone trying to help me sort through the devastation I had experienced. God placed people around me to envelope me with the love

I needed to get through this. But the loneliness was almost unbearable. I knew I was in a spiritual attack like none I had ever experienced.

In church one Sunday morning the following June, the Lord spoke to me through my Pastor's sermon. Pastor made the statement that you can't fully embrace what God has for your future if you don't turn lose of your past. He even said that you may have lost a loved one and haven't been able to go on.

It was at that moment that the Holy Spirit spoke to my heart about resuming my stand of faith for a godly mate by getting back on eHarmony. I told the Lord I didn't want to do that; I would just be content with being single the rest of my life. But He kept reminding me that He had promised me a godly mate and He would bring that into manifestation. But I had to do my part and that was to place myself in the position to meet the man He would bring into my life.

On the weekend of July 4th, a man by the name of Gerald came up. His profile matched mine on my eHarmony match list. I told the Lord if this was the man I was to meet then he would have to contact me because I wasn't going to initiate the contact. I waited. On July 13th, Gerald contacted me. We went through all the preliminary questions from eHarmony within just a few days.

Gerald had never been married and was also praying for a godly mate. We decided to talk by phone since we both had many questions to be answered. In a seven hour phone conversation all the important issues were discussed and we felt God leading us to meet.

Gerald paid all my expenses to fly to Tennessee where he lived and to stay in a motel for several days. He treated me like a queen, and I thoroughly enjoyed it! He was a perfect gentleman and a truly godly man.

Gerald and I were married on October 11, 2008, in his backyard overlooking the valleys of Tennessee. God placed in my life the man that He had chosen for me and every one of the specifications for a godly mate that I had written down was in Gerald. He has and continues to be my gift from God. God took what I had seen as the devastation of my life and turned it around for good ". . . <u>But God</u>!" He had done what I considered the impossible....once again. "Thank you, Lord God, for Gerald, my special gift from You."

Be still, let go, cease striving, relax,
and know that I am God!

Psalm 46:10 (Expanded Version)

19. <u>It Pays to Listen and Obey</u>

(From Sue)

A few months ago I was prepping messages for our conference. We were four weeks away but couldn't seem to 'hear' a thing from God about what the content of the messages should be. Panic was beginning to set in since there was so much to do yet in such a short time.

One day I was at my friend's home when an overwhelming sense to lay aside everything and just 'be' with the Lord came to me. I ignored it because I had to get some work done. A little while later the same thought nudged me again since I was unable to get anything done. By day's end, I was very frustrated from not having accomplished anything. Two days later, I felt so drawn to get back to the home like a magnet. I knew this time the Lord had something in store. So this time I listened, just sat, prayed, and worshipped.

I was so thankful I was alone. For what began as a simple prayer turned into a full-fledged, heavy, deliberate, intense something! It went on for about two hours. When I was able to get up off the floor even I didn't know what had just happened.

Two days later, I went to my friends' house again, only this time, they were home and helping me with some of the subject matter. Once again, we weren't making any progress, so she said, "Susan, we just need to stop, drop, and pray."

I hate it when the obvious is soooo simple and I didn't think of it! Again, I began to pray and again there was something developing in me. Before I knew it, I was praying something (even I hadn't heard that 'tone' in me before.) This wasn't a normal time of prayer. Again, after pulling myself up off the floor, I began to see little Scrabble-like pieces begin to drop into my head.

I began to hear, "Tell His Story-- tell HISTORY, tell HIS STORY--from Creator to Savior over and over again." At the same time I began searching for a note pad to write what I was seeing and hearing in my head. As God gave them to me, I wrote the Names of God, from Creator to Savior, in the order of how they are given in the Bible as God continued to reveal Himself.

In that pattern, there were seven. It was as if I was being given the story of how each name led to the next. For example: The God who Created us saw us, and because He saw us He knew we needed a Provider, Shepherd, Healer, Comforter, Savior, etc. When I came to, for lack of a better word, I saw my friend who had been sitting behind me the whole time.

Have you ever had one of those moments where you feel a little awkward and look around to see if someone just saw you? I felt like that at that moment. Anyway, after a minute or two my friend just looked at me and with tears running down her face asked me if I knew what I had been praying?

I assumed I was just praying. She then picked up a book and put it in my lap. God had given me His Names in the order they were to be preached, and I had been praying them in Hebrew. As I saw them "drop" as Scrabble pieces into English, apparently I was praying them in the Hebrew tongue. So needless to say the rest of the preparation for the conference went off without a hitch ". . . <u>But God!</u>" It pays to listen and obey!

God, Who gives us richly all things to enjoy.

I Timothy 6:17b NKJV

20. <u>The Stained Glass Window</u>

(By Karen Joy King)

The other day, a friend invited me to provide music for their church camp out, which was held at her church. I hadn't been to her church for thirteen years. She had told me they had built a new church next door to the small old one but had no idea what it looked like. When I arrived, my mouth hung open in awe at the new structure and landscaping. It was absolutely breath-takingly beautiful AND huge!

Before I did the music program, I told the pastor that my church, where I was attending at that time, was in the process of building a new church, and I would like to talk to him about his new church and the experiences he had. He gladly and enthusiastically gave me a tour. Every part of the church was so well planned and laid out, and did I mention –HUGE? The old church would fit into just the narthex, and it is only a congregation of around 140 people.

The pastor shared with me how God had blessed them in so many ways so they could have the new church and the grounds around it, including a large day care. There was one stained glass window in the whole church, but it was an eye catcher. I mentioned how beautiful it was to the pastor. He smiled broadly and told me the ". . .<u>But God!</u>" story about it.

Around the time the new church was being planned, the pastor had driven through a certain area and had noticed this stained glass window in a salvage store display. He stopped to ask about it since it had captured his attention. The owner related to him that there had been a church out west which had been torn down due to a new highway going straight through it. He had bought 25 of these beautiful windows from the church and had sold 24 of them. He explained to the pastor that for some reason, he had kept this one window back and had pulled it out of storage just that morning. It had only been on display a few hours before the pastor had arrived.

The pastor told the store owner, by faith, to put a "sold" sign on the window and that he would be back shortly to pick it up. When the pastor arrived back home and shared with some of the church people about the window, the amount he needed to buy the window was immediately given to him, and he picked it up.

That story in itself is amazing enough, but there is more. That evening, a drunk driver ran his truck into the store window where the stained glass window had been and demolished the store front.

God coordinated the timing of the window being brought out for display with the pastor's arrival and church people who had money on the spot to give to the pastor in order for him to pick it up at the right time. God's timing is always perfect. ". . . But God!"

The pastor said he built the new church around the stained glass window since it was the gospel in a nut shell.

When you pass through the waters,
I will be with you
And through the rivers, they shall
not overflow you.
When you walk through the fire,
you shall not be burned,
Nor will the flame scorch you.
Isaiah 43:2 NKJV

21. <u>A Fire Forced Us From Our Home</u>

(From Lael)

One of the smaller wildfires here in Arizona forced us out of our home. We had time to pack a small school bus with our belongings, get our cats, and go to my parents' house. The winds were very strong and the fire had come within a mile of us before it turned back on itself. (We had all our friends specifically praying that the winds would shift and turn the fire on itself, and that's just what happened. Praise God! ". . . <u>But God</u>!"

We stayed away for a number of days until the fire was under control in our area and the smoke had cleared; and, thankfully, went home to find our house still standing. I am still bringing back small loads of stuff to the house and reorganizing as I go. God is really good! I find He is using it to help me pare down, decide what is important, what isn't, and simplify our lives. That is a really good thing.

Our house sits at the edge of the Coronado National Forest with views to the west of three small mountain ranges. We are used to spring winds, and as the heat rises they usually become soft breezes at best. However, this May and early June, the winds were unusually high and continued day in and day out for weeks; so, once it started, the fire was very difficult to control.

It began burning to the northwest of us in the Tumacacori Mountains; and, as we watched daily, it burned its way south and east toward the Atascosa Mountains -- and our house. The winds were blowing the smoke northward even though the fire was moving steadily south. For quite a long time, we didn't have the smell of smoke in spite of the proximity of the fire.

The fire crews couldn't get in to fight the wildest parts of the fire because the terrain was so difficult; so, they concentrated their efforts on creating fire lines and protecting the communities knowing they would have to allow the mountains burn. That was worrisome since we live only a short distance from the base of the mountains and were watching the flames grow larger and closer every day. We set up watches at night and would regularly check on where it was in case we needed to leave.

As it came within a mile of us, we asked all our friends and families to pray with us so the winds would shift and the fire would begin to burn back on itself and spare the town and us. At about the same time, we were given a pre-evacuation notice and began packing our cats and things we couldn't replace.

The night we were packing, all of a sudden, the fire laid down and the winds stopped. Unfortunately, that meant the smoke all of a sudden laid down as well and ash settled all around our house. It choked us so badly that we packed up very quickly and left. For the next two days the winds would pick up during the day and stop at night, so, we watched from afar, kept our eyes on the incident reports as the crews battled to keep the fire line from being breached, and continued to pray with family and friends.

On the third day, the winds shifted in the opposite direction and the fire quickly began to burn itself out around the populated areas. Our house was spared along with all the houses in our town; and, in spite of the danger to the fire crews, there were no significant injuries to anyone. All three of the mountain ranges to our southwest, west, and northwest were completely burned right to their bases; and, in some cases, quite close to the community.

My immediate reflection on all this was that I had found it surprisingly easy to leave most of our belongings behind knowing it was possible they would be burned up in the fire. There was a sense of freedom I got from simply letting go of it all and trusting that God had our good in mind no matter what the outcome might be.

I realized it was an opportunity to simplify our lives and God had graciously given us clear dividing lines. Without being touched by the flames, I experienced a measure of the cleansing power of fire even as we thanked God for His hand that stayed its course. We have been so aware that only God stood between us and the flames for nearly two weeks. He was in control of what was touched by them, and we are so thankful to Him for His merciful hand.

I fully expected to return home to the smell of smoke throughout the house; but, when we did return, not even the smell of smoke was in and around the house. God literally kept us through it all and left no trace or smell of smoke in the end ". . . <u>But God</u>!"

Trust in the Lord with all your heart,

And lean not on your own understanding;

In all your ways acknowledge Him,

And He shall direct your paths.

Proverbs 3:5, 6 NKJV

22. Father, Take the Wheel

(By Karen Joy King)

Many years ago, a young lady author was learning to trust God as her mother had tried to teach her. She was returning home from a speaking engagement late one night and since it had been a long dreary winter trip, she was tired and feeling discouraged. But before going home, she knew she should stop at a drugstore to pick up some needed medicine before reaching her home.

The street where she parked was very busy, so as to not hold up traffic, she slid out the right side of the car. When she got home, she noticed that her favorite little blue velvet hat was missing. She figured that since it had been on the seat beside her it must have fallen into the street when she had gotten out of the car.

She wanted to drive back right then and look for her hat, but it was cold and dark and knew she was too tired to safely do so; so she asked God to protect her little hat which was lying on a very busy street. "Please, Father, protect it for me until morning. I thank, You, with all my heart." There, she thought, that little prayer would please my mother!

Having given her burden about her hat to God, she slept well and in the morning drove back to get it. She parked the car where she had the previous day, and when she looked down the street, there was the little blue hat in perfect condition ". . . <u>But God</u>!"

The Blue Hat
Drawn by Heidi Smith

It was a miracle for cars had continuously been driving in that spot since the previous day. She thought, "If God could care enough to protect a little hat, how much more would He care to protect me?" How wonderful it was to be able to pray, simply take her hands off the situation, and let God work!

This same young lady was again returning from another long speaking trip. She had stayed in a pastor's home; and upon leaving, the pastor's wife prayed that God would protect her return trip home. "Dear God, please protect her. Don't let anything happen to her, and lead her safely to her loved ones."

She had only driven thirty miles when it began sleeting and freezing. She drove slowly but a truck in front of her slowed her even more. When she came to a place she thought she could safely pass, she started to go around the truck but lost control of her car. All she could think about was a horrific accident since there were a lot of cars behind her and the truck beside her. She wondered if she would be severely hurt or even killed. Then she remembered the pastor's wife's prayer for her safety and prayed, "I can't drive, Father. Take the wheel."

Hardly before her prayer had ended, her car was setting on an uphill bank by the road facing the opposite direction. The truck driver had stopped and came to her to see if she was all right. When he found that she was, he stated that it was a miracle that she was since her car had barely missed his truck and that the other cars behind her had been able to stop.

He asked, "How could you get control of the car and drive it onto the bank?" The young lady felt foolish, but told him that she had prayed, simply let go of the wheel, and had let God drive the car ". . .<u>But God</u>!" The truck driver and several other drivers were able to lift her car off the embankment and onto the road. She continued her journey and arrived home safely.

The Lord is my Shepherd, I shall not want.

Psalm 23:1 NKJV

23. "I Want You to Brush His Hair"

(This story was originally in *A Heart Like His* by Beth Moore [Published by LifeWay in 1996]. This Bible study, *A Heart Like His,* was updated in 2010. The story is now found on Disc 1 in the Bible study *David: Seeking A Heart Like His* by Beth Moore published by LifeWay Christian Resources.)

For those of you who do not know Beth Moore, she is an outstanding Bible teacher, writer of Bible studies, and is a married mother of two daughters. This is one of her . . . ". . . But God!" experiences in her words, which she said anyone could share.

April 20, 2005, at the Airport in Knoxville, waiting to board the plane, I had the Bible on my lap and was very intent upon what I was doing. I'd had a marvelous morning with the Lord. I say this because I want to tell you it is a scary thing to have the Spirit of God really working in you. You could end up doing some things you never would have done otherwise. Life in the Spirit can be dangerous for a thousand reasons, not the least of which is your ego.

I tried to keep from staring, but he was such a strange sight. Humped over in a wheelchair, he was skin and bones, dressed in clothes that obviously fit when he was at least twenty pounds heavier. His knees protruded from his trousers, and his shoulders looked like the coat hanger was still in his shirt. His hands looked like tangled masses of veins and bones.

The strangest part of him was his hair and nails. Stringy, gray hair hung well over his shoulders and down part of his back. His fingernails were long, clean but strangely out of place on an old man.

I looked down at my Bible as fast as I could, discomfort burning my face. As I tried to imagine what his story might have been, I found myself wondering if I'd just had a Howard Hughes sighting. Then, I remembered that he was dead. So this man in the airport ... an impersonator maybe? Was a camera on us somewhere? There I sat; trying to concentrate on the Word to keep from being concerned about a thin slice of humanity served up on a wheelchair only a few seats from me.

All the while, my heart was growing more and more overwhelmed with a feeling for him. Let's admit it. Curiosity is a heap more comfortable than true concern, and suddenly I was awash with aching emotion for this bizarre-looking old man.

I had walked with God long enough to see the handwriting on the wall. I've learned that when I begin to feel what God feels, something so contrary to my natural feelings, something dramatic is bound to happen. And it may be embarrassing.

I immediately began to resist because I could feel God working on my spirit and I started arguing with God in my mind. 'Oh, no, God, please, no.' I looked up at the ceiling as if I could stare straight through it into heaven and said, 'Don't make me witness to this man. Not right here and now. Please. I'll do anything. Put me on the same plane, but don't make me get up here and witness to this man in front of this gawking audience. Please, Lord!'

There I sat in the blue vinyl chair begging His Highness, 'Please don't make me witness to this man. Not now. I'll do it on the plane.' Then I heard it... 'I don't want you to witness to him. I want you to brush his hair.'

The words were so clear, my heart leapt into my throat, and my thoughts spun like a top. Do I witness to the man or brush his hair? No-brainer. I looked straight back up at the ceiling and said, 'God, as I live and breathe, I want you to know I am ready to witness to this man. I'm on this Lord. I'm your girl! You've never seen a woman witness to a man faster in your life. What difference does it make if his hair is a mess if he is not redeemed? I am going to witness to this man.'

Again, as clearly as I've ever heard an audible word, God seemed to write this statement across the wall of my mind. 'That is not what I said, Beth. I don't want you to witness to him. I want you to go brush his hair.'

I looked up at God and quipped, I don't have a hairbrush. It's in my suitcase on the plane. How am I supposed to brush his hair without a hairbrush?' God was so insistent that I almost involuntarily began to walk toward him as these thoughts came to me from God's word: 'I will thoroughly furnish you unto all good works.' (2 Timothy 3:17)

I stumbled over to the wheelchair thinking I could use one myself. Even as I retell this story, my pulse quickens and I feel those same butterflies. I knelt down in front of the man and asked as demurely as possible, 'Sir, May I have the pleasure of brushing your hair?'

He looked back at me and said, 'What did you say?'

'May I have the pleasure of brushing your hair?'

To which he responded in volume ten, 'Little lady, if you expect me to hear you, you're going to have to talk louder than that.'

At this point, I took a deep breath and blurted out, 'SIR, MAY I HAVE THE PLEASURE OF BRUSHING YOUR HAIR?' At which point every eye in the place darted right at me. I was the only thing in the room looking more peculiar than old Mr. Long Locks. Face crimson and forehead breaking out in a sweat, I watched him look up at me with absolute shock on his face, and say, 'If you really want to.'

Are you kidding? Of course I didn't want to. But God didn't seem interested in my personal preference right about then. He pressed on my heart until I could utter the words, 'Yes, sir, I would be pleased. But I have one little problem. I don't have a hairbrush.' 'I have one in my bag,' he responded.

I went around to the back of that wheelchair, and I got on my hands and knees and unzipped the stranger's old carry-on, hardly believing what I was doing. I stood up and started brushing the old man's hair.

It was perfectly clean, but it was tangled and matted. I don't do many things well, but must admit I've had notable experience untangling knotted hair mothering two little girls. Like I'd done with either Amanda or Melissa in such a condition, I began brushing at the very bottom of the strands, remembering to take my time not to pull.

A miraculous thing happened to me as I started brushing that old man's hair. Everybody else in the room disappeared. There was no one alive for those moments except that old man and me. I brushed and I brushed and I brushed until every tangle was out of that hair. I know this sounds so strange, but I've never felt that kind of love for another soul in my entire life. I believe with all my heart, I for that few minutes felt a portion of the very love of God. That He had overtaken my heart for a little while like someone renting a room and making Himself at home for a short while ". . . But God!"

The emotions were so strong and so pure that I knew they had to be God's. His hair was finally as soft and smooth as an infant's. I slipped the brush back in the bag and went around the chair to face him. I got back down on my knees, put my hands on his knee and said,'Sir, do you know my Jesus?' He said, 'Yes, I do.' Well, that figures, I thought.

He explained, 'I've known Him since I married my bride. She wouldn't marry me until I got to know the Savior.' He said, 'You see, the problem is, I haven't seen my bride in months. I've had open-heart surgery, and she's been too ill to come see me. I was sitting here thinking to myself, what a mess I must be for my bride.'

Only God knows how often He allows us to be part of a divine moment when we're completely unaware of the significance. This, on the other hand, was one of those rare encounters when I knew God had intervened in details only He could have known. It was a God moment, and I'll never forget it.

Our time came to board, and we were not on the same plane. I was deeply ashamed of how I'd acted earlier and would have been so proud to have accompanied him on that aircraft. I still had a few minutes, and as I gathered my things to board, the airline hostess returned from the corridor, tears streaming down her cheeks. She said, 'That old man's sitting on the plane, sobbing. Why did you do that? What made you do that?'

I said, 'Do you know Jesus? He can be the bossiest thing!' And we got to share.

I learned something about God that day. He knows if you're exhausted, you're hungry, you're serving in the wrong place or it is time to move on but you feel too responsible to budge. He knows if you're hurting or feeling rejected. He knows if you're sick or drowning under a wave of temptation. Or He knows if you just need your hair brushed. He sees you as an individual. Tell Him your need!

I got on my own flight, sobs choking my throat, wondering how many opportunities just like that one had I missed along the way... all because I didn't want people to think I was strange. God didn't send me to that old man. He sent that old man to me. Please share this wonderful story.

'Life isn't about how to survive the storm, but how to dance in the rain!'

So the sun stood still, and the moon stopped,
  Till the people had revenge upon their
        enemies.

Joshua 10:13 NKJV

24. <u>Isn't It Amazing?</u>

<u>(Paraphrased from Joshua 10 and II Kings 20)</u>

(By Karen Joy King)

Several stories from the Bible have always amazed me. One is of Joshua telling the sun and moon to stand still so he could finish fighting his enemy; and the other is when King Hezekiah was given a sign that he would live and asked that the sun reverse its shadow by ten degrees. Both of these miracles together constitute the loss of one whole day.

<u>From Joshua 10</u>

The Israelites had entered into their land of promise, but there were many enemies to fight. Five kings and their armies came against the Israelites. It was going to be a big battle, but the Lord said to Joshua, 'Fear them not, I have delivered them into your hand; there shall not a man of them stand before you.' What an encouraging word!

After marching his army all night for an attack upon these kings, Joshua came upon the enemy. Just as they were to engage the battle, the Lord stepped in and routed the enemy killing many of them with a great slaughter. Israel began to chase the enemy. As they did, the Lord once again fought for Israel and killed many more with large hail stones from heaven.

Since the battle was far from over, Joshua knew he needed more time to finish it, so he commanded the sun and the moon to stand still! That's right! Who would think that a mere man could have so much boldness and power? It came from the Lord!

Joshua Commanding Sun To Stand Still
Drawn by Heidi Smith

'The sun stood still and the moon stayed and lasted not to go down about a whole day (twenty-three hours and twenty minutes)." (Joshua 10:12-13)

This was a mighty miracle ". . . <u>But God</u>!" Think of it! The earth and the moon actually standing still! Given that much extra daylight, Joshua, with God's intervention, was able to defeat those kings and their armies!

<u>From II Kings 20</u>

King Hezekiah was sick and dying, so the prophet Isaiah told him to get his house in order. However, the king didn't want to die, so he turned his face to the wall and prayed, "Remember now, O Lord, I pray, how I have walked before You in truth and with a loyal heart, and have done what was good in Your sight."

This is a good pattern for us to follow when petitioning God – to remind Him of how we have walked with Him. Even though God already knows, it still helps to get His attention. God heard and immediately answered. Isaiah was stopped in his tracks as he was leaving the king for He told him to go back and to tell him that the Lord had heard his prayer. God promised to heal Hezekiah and to add fifteen years to his life.

Hezekiah wanted to believe this so he asked for a sign from the Lord. (In those days, God spoke through prophets instead of directly to people). Isaiah told him that God was giving him a choice. Did he want the sun to go forward ten degrees or backward ten degrees? The king reasoned, 'It is nothing for the sun to go ahead ten degrees, but let the shadow return backward ten degrees.' So, Isaiah asked the Lord to do this, and the sun went backward ten degrees (forty minutes).

Just as God promised, Hezekiah was healed and lived another fifteen years ". . . <u>But God</u>!"

Twenty-three hours and twenty minutes for Joshua, plus forty minutes for Hezekiah make a whole day which many scientists claim is missing in the universe's time clock! Isn't it amazing? ". . . <u>But God</u>!"

Who forgives all your iniquities,
Who heals all your diseases,
Who redeems your life from destruction.

Psalm 103:3, 4 NKJV

25. The Sword Was Pulled Out of Her Back

(By Karen Joy King)

I love to hear stories about people healed by God's power. I have laid hands on and prayed over several people myself and have seen them healed. Sometimes, I pray with people over the phone or via emails and live chats. I have no power in myself but use the authority Jesus has given me through His powerful name. "That at the name of Jesus every knee must bow, of those in heaven, and of those on earth, and of those under the earth, and that every tongue should confess that Jesus Christ is Lord, to the glory of God the Father." (Philippians 2:10, 11)

Another scripture I take seriously is found in the Great Commission, "Go into all the world and preach the gospel to every creature. He who believes and is baptized will be saved; but he does not believe will be condemned. And these signs will follow those who believe; in my name they will cast out demons; they will speak with new tongues; they will take up serpents; and if they drink anything deadly, it will by no means hurt them; they will lay hands on the sick, and they will recover." (Mark 16:15-18)

Another favorite is John 14:12-14, "Most assuredly, I say to you, he who believes in Me, the works that I do, he will do also, and greater works than these he will do, because I go to the Father. And whatever you ask in My name, that I will do, that the Father may be glorified in the Son. If you ask anything in My name, I will do it."

One of my Christian Leadership University students experienced a miraculous healing which I want to share along with explaining a little about God's sovereignty.

God has sovereignty over nature. Nature is under God's law. He set these laws in place, and nature must obey. He created it all and it is under His rule and set all of it in place. He told the oceans where to stop and they obey. Since God set up the laws and boundaries, He is completely sovereign and can choose at any time to move outside of these boundaries. He can work a miracle that completely defies the natural laws of nature.

The Bible is full of these miracle-breaking incidents which overcome the laws of our natural world. God worked powerful miracles to show Himself great to His people, the Israelites. Jesus worked many miracles, showing that He was Lord over the laws of nature.

Today He still does this. He brought just such a healing miracle to the life of my student (and many others), for which she is so thankful! Her back had gotten to the place where her last resort was to see a specialist since she had been dealing with severe pain for a month and the medication hadn't given her any relief.

One night, her family got together to pray for her. During prayer, she saw (in the Spirit) a sword being pulled out of her back. When she stood up, all of the pain was gone!!!!! ". . . <u>But God!</u>" God had defied the laws of nature and had removed her pain!

Her testimony included, "I know that God is ruling, but it amazes me how often I act like I am the one in charge. Many times I forget to check with God and get in His way. I want to be totally submitted to Him so I can accomplish His will at all times and in all places."

Joseph of the Bible is such an inspirational story along these lines. We should all want to be able to trust God like this young man even though his circumstances went from bad to worse. Joseph kept the faith and a right attitude through it all and God blessed him. He didn't allow bitterness in his life because of the hurtful things done to him. Eventually, God raised him from the dungeon to the throne.

God is also sovereign over His decree. God determined what He would accomplish through His creation so His eternal purpose would be fulfilled. He is orchestrating everything to accomplish His design that He laid out from the foundation of the earth. Sometimes we may think that the world is out of control but God knows the end from the beginning and will go according to His plan.

The Bible says that God knew Adam would sin, so it didn't take Him by surprise when he did, for He had already made provision in His plan to redeem mankind. God is, and always will be in control. God's decree can also be stated as His purpose for His pleasure.

The Father wants us to know His pleasure and His will for our lives. He longs to reveal to us why we are here and what His plans for our lives are. We are made for His glory, it is all about God glorifying Himself through us for our lives are not our own.

God desires to bring all into His glory through His Son, Jesus. Jesus paid the ultimate price through His great suffering and horrible death on the cross so we can be saved from eternal death, if we will only accept Him.

God is sovereign over the flow of history. It is so amazing to see God's hand throughout history. Often we only have the perspective that man messes things up for God all the time. Yes, man does mess things up when he is not submitted to God and seeking to do His will, but God is not surprised at any time by man's actions. Ultimately, God's plan will be accomplished, culminating at the end of this age with God using the wicked nations to play a part in His second coming!

Throughout history, God raised up kingdoms for His purpose and when He was done with them, He deposed of them. Wicked people and rulers may appear to have the upper hand for now, but not so – God always does! Even the Antichrist will be a tool in the hand of the Lord! We cannot afford to allow any disobedience in our lives for the coming of the Lord is very, very soon. Be watching and ready. Even so, Lord Jesus, come quickly!

He was wounded for our transgressions,
He was bruised for our iniquities;
The chastisement for our peace was upon Him,
By His stripes we are healed.

Isaiah 53:5 NKJV

26. <u>Piano Teacher Healed</u>

(By Karen Joy King)

Another wonderful healing story is about a piano teacher who taught one of my students's daughter. My student had bought the Christian Leadership University books for one of the healing courses. After reading them, plus years of learning from her pastors; through her prayer, God performed a healing miracle.

The piano teacher had scoliosis and two big curved vertebrae on top of each other. The student said, "As I prayed for her, she could feel her vertebrae straighten up. Her hip, which is usually twisted and lop-sided about seven inches, also adjusted and became straight. Then one of her legs grew two inches in order to be the same as the other ". . . <u>But God!</u>"

Jesus healed all who came to Him when He was on earth, and now He heals through His followers, those who trust in Him and have made Him their Lord and Savior. "And by His stripes we are healed." (Isaiah 53:5b) "For with God nothing will be impossible." (Luke 1:37)

No good thing will He withhold

from those who walk uprightly!

Psalm 84:11 NKJV

27. <u>God Provided for Two Houses</u>

(By Karen Joy King)

In 1992, recently divorced, too sick to earn a decent living, and having only $5000 to my name, I had been living with various people over the years and desired to have my own home. This became a serious matter of prayer for me. Through different realtors, I searched for a home I could afford (yeah right!), but I kept praying and looking anyway.

A house and lot near where I was living at the time was on the market and its price had been dropped several times until it was only $32,500 (still a lot more than I had), but I checked it out.

Of course I would need a loan, but none of the banks would even consider giving me one since my income was practically nil. After a lot of prayer, I tried one last area bank, and they gave me the loan with a down payment of $4995. This left me with $5. By faith, I felt God wanted me to have this house and that He would enable me to make the payments and meet all the other bills -- utilities, insurance, upkeep, and my own personal needs – and He miraculously did!

I never missed a house payment or any other payment. He even enabled me to earn enough money to fix it up and make a nice home out of it, although it wasn't that bad before, for it was a good solid home. Through these various fixer-upper projects, I learned to roof, to plumb, do electrical, put on vinyl siding, do dry-wall, install carpet, put up paneling and ceiling tile, build a stair banister, and add a large deck. This was a lot of fun and very fulfilling for me since I like new challenges.

At the end of 1999, I had to sell this house and move in with my elderly mother on the family farm to take care of her due to her failing health and losing her eye sight. Since I had fixed up the house, I was able to sell it for over double the purchase price (truly a ". . . <u>But God!</u>" thing since I had listed it above the bank's price).

With this money, I was able to pay off the remainder of my house loan, college loan, purchase a nicer car, and had money to put in the bank towards another home after my mother's death.

When my mother died, my brothers and I sold the family farm. From what I had saved, besides my house sale money and my inheritance, I was able to purchase outright a very nice home, which is another story.

One night while I was trying to go to sleep when still at the farm (by this time, Mom had been in the nursing home for several years), God suddenly asked me, "What kind of house would you like?" I thought for a little while and then answered Him, "Since I am getting older and need something easy to take care of, I would like a one-story ranch style house with a two car attached garage, just enough yard to be nice, and a yard shed."

The reason I wanted a one-story was because my other house and the farm house were two-stories and it took a lot of effort to keep them up. The reason I wanted just a nice sized lot was because it took me four and a half hours to mow at the family farm. The reason I wanted an attached garage was because at my former house and at the farm, there was distance between the houses and garages.

When Mom died and the farm was put up for sale, I had to find a new home very quickly. I didn't want to go into debt, so I looked at homes within a certain price range. Quite by accident (not really, it was a ". . . But God!" thing again), while looking at another home, which I wasn't really interested in but just wanted to see it, I came across a house I had gone by many times and it always drew my attention because it was so neat and cute.

Low and behold, it was for sale. I had no idea this place was for sale and automatically assumed that it was more than I could afford; however, I couldn't get it off my mind, so I called the owner and found the price had just been lowered to within my price range. It was even nicer than the dream house I had told God I wanted. Isn't that just like God – to give beyond my expectation? ". . . But God!"

Call to Me, and I will answer you,
and show you great and mighty things,
which you do not know.

Jeremiah 33:3 NKJV

28. <u>Technically Challenged</u>

(By Karen Joy King)

Being technically challenged, I was totally at a loss when I inserted a DVD into my VCR/DVD player and changed the TV channel to 03 as normal, but the screen came up for "Language" instead of for playing DVD's, and I couldn't get off that screen. I checked the wiring. It was ok. I tried changing channels and reinserting the DVD – nothing worked.

Finally, I prayed, "Father, You have promised to be better to me than any earthly father and husband. You know I don't have the faintest idea what to do, and You just told me to watch this DVD (a training DVD for my university). Please show me what to do. Thank You, in Jesus' Name. Amen"

My ". . . <u>But God!</u>" moment came as God told me to press the "DVD" button on my remote. I pressed it, and immediately, the DVD was ready to play.

I know, many of you could have figured that out easily; but like I said, I am technically challenged and that is the reason I rely upon my heavenly Father to help me. This isn't the first time I have sought God's help for something nor will it be the last, for I rely heavily upon Him for everything in my life.

He wants to do the same for you. If you have a need, quiet yourself before Him, focus on Him, and be ready to receive once you have asked Him in faith. His voice usually comes as a spontaneous thought, word, idea, or picture. However, if you are not quiet or in faith, it is easy to miss His voice. (See the Appendix for further explanation.) Be sure to thank Him and worship Him in the process, for praise will bring Him quickly into your situation.

Ask, and it will be given to you

Matthew 7:7 NKJV

29. <u>God's Answer to Prayer</u>

(From Connie Eberly)

Both my husband and I have health problems which keeps us from earning a good income. Both our truck and car were old, and the car was to the point we were scared to drive it. I had been praying for over a year about how to replace the car since we didn't have the money to do it.

One day a friend called and very hesitantly asked, "Connie, would you accept a different vehicle if I got it for you?" I began to cry and said, "Yes, I have been praying about this. This is an answer to my prayer!" My friend told me that God had been speaking to her heart for around a year about buying us a better vehicle and that she had been really impressed to do so now.

My friend called around to different dealers and located some vehicles in the price range she could afford. Upon finding several at a certain dealer, she asked us to meet her there and pick out the vehicle we wanted.

Both my husband I held our breath and prayed all the way to the dealer in hopes that our car would make it. Once there, we looked over the vehicles and found a nice van which we both loved. Our friend paid for it, and we were able to drive home in our answer-to-prayer vehicle! This was a great big ". . . <u>But God</u>!" for us!

Be sober, be vigilant, because your adversary
the devil walks about like a roaring lion,
seeking whom he may devour.

I Peter 5:8 NKJV

30. <u>Believe it or Not, There is a Devil</u>

(By Karen Joy King)

For those of you who don't believe there is a devil and a host of demons, you'd better think again. They are as real as you and I, and very powerful, but not anywhere as powerful as God. They constantly go about seeking whom they can destroy. (I Peter 5:8)

As believers, God gave us authority over them. We are told in God's word to submit ourselves to God, to resist the devil, and he will flee from us. (James 4:7) He comes at us in all kinds of ways so we must stay alert and discern him.

The following is one incident in which I encountered him (of course I have had many more). One Sunday morning while I was playing the organ at church, suddenly it felt like something grabbed my left leg and caused it to shake like a nervous tremor.

At that time, due to some health issues, I had been having trouble with my nerves whenever I tried to do any music at church, both vocally and instrumentally.

Sometimes, I would start shaking so much I could hardly finish the musical number. So while on the organ bench that morning, I thought it was just another case of nerves, yet it seemed different.

After I got home and was thinking and praying about the incident, God showed me that a demon had grabbed my leg. At that moment, I took authority over the demon of nervousness, rebuked it, and told it through Jesus' name to never touch me again. Since then, I no longer experience nervousness shaking when playing an instrument or singing. Praise the Lord ". . . But God!"

When any kind of negativity or cloud comes upon you, take authority over it and command it to leave in the Name of Jesus. Then ask God to restore whatever the demon has stolen from you.

Sometimes, the demonic intruder is very evident and easy to identify, but if you are not sure, pause and ask God the name of the demonic spirit so you can address it specifically. A couple Biblical examples are found in:

Luke 4:33-35, "In the synagogue there was a man possessed by the spirit of an unclean demon, and he cried out with a loud voice, 'Let us alone! What business do we have with each other, Jesus of Nazareth? Have You come to destroy us? I know who You are—the Holy One of God!' But Jesus rebuked him, saying, 'Be quiet and come out of him!' And when the demon had thrown him down in the midst of the people, he came out of him without doing him any harm."

Acts 16:16-18, "It happened that as we were going to the place of prayer, a slave-girl having a spirit of divination met us, who was bringing her masters much profit by fortune-telling. Following after Paul and us, she kept crying out, saying, 'These men are bond-servants of the Most High God, who are proclaiming to you the way of salvation.' She continued doing this for many days. But Paul was greatly annoyed, and turned and said to the spirit, 'I command you in the name of Jesus Christ to come out of her!' And it came out at that very moment."

There is no way a Christian can be demon-possessed but they can have demonic strongholds which can trouble them. Any area of a Christian's life that the Christian doesn't have victory over should be explored through the Holy Spirit to find out what the stronghold is. By taking the steps Paul did, these strongholds can be broken. Once they are broken, immediately ask the Holy Spirit to fill the void.

Followers of Christ can expect to be attacked for Satan hates us. I Peter 5:8-9, "Be of a sober spirit, be on the alert. Your adversary, the devil, prowls around like a roaring lion, seeking someone to devour. But resist him, firm in your faith, knowing that the same experiences of suffering are being accomplished by your brethren who are in the world."

Since Satan is watching for any opportunity to attack us, we need to be careful of what we agree with. He is cunning, subtle, a thief, a murderer, an accuser, and a liar. Scripture warns us that unresolved emotional issues can create spiritual strongholds in a Christian's life. If you are having problems in any area of your life, ask God to reveal the demon causing it, then take authority over it, break any agreement you may have with it, and cast it out in the name of Jesus. It is always wise to ask God how to deal with it step by step, for He knows exactly the issue and how to overcome it. Jesus died so that we may have abundant life in Him. (John 10:10) He doesn't want us living in any kind of bondage.

Be of a good courage

and He shall strengthen your heart,

All you who hope in the Lord.

Psalm 31:24 NKJV

31. <u>The Hope We Have in Christ</u>

(From Pastor Bob Waggoner)

I first met my beautiful wife, Betty, in 1950. After an eleven month courtship, we married in 1951. One of the precious things about our wedding was that God showed us through His Word that our wedding was His will for us.

We have had a wonderful 59 years of wedded life. As I look back, I can only say that God had led us over the years for which we were together, and I am grateful to Him since we have had so many wonderful memories.

About three years ago (at the time of this writing), Betty broke her hip. After her surgery, we had to place her in a nursing home where her health continued to fail. On October 1, 2010, when a worker at the home started to get her up that morning, she noticed that Betty was having difficulty breathing.

Betty's memory had been affected for some time and she could no longer speak in sentences, usually only a word once in a while. The worker reported that Betty spoke two sentences, "Hi, how are you doing?" and then, "What a beautiful day to be with the Lord." A big smile broke out on Betty's face, and she was gone. The worker said that at the moment of Betty's death, it was something she had never experienced before. She felt it was caused by the unseen presence of the angel who had come to escort Betty to heaven. Wow! What a home going! Praise the Lord!

My only tears have been tears of joy, and I know that it won't be long until I see her again since I truly believe the Rapture (when God calls His saints to heaven just before the seven year tribulation takes place) is very close at hand. (See the book of Revelation).

As I look back over the years, I have so much to be grateful for to God by His bringing Betty into my life. He gave us seven wonderful children and 59 happy years together. Her time at the nursing home not only opened up ministries, but was a reflection of the love of God as she was known there as a "sweet woman." We have enjoyed many ". . .<u>But God!</u>" moments throughout our lives. My dear wife Betty has been accepted by the Lord and is now enjoying living in His presence.

Some scripture which has been very meaningful to us is: "For we know that if our earthly house of this tabernacle were dissolved, we have a building of God, a house not made with hands, eternal in the heavens. Therefore, we are always confident, knowing that, while we are at home in the body, we are absent from the Lord: (For we walk by faith, not by sight): We are confident, I say, and willing rather to be absent from the body and to be present with the Lord. Wherefore we labor, that whether present or absent, we may be accepted of Him." (2nd Corinthians 5:1, 6-9)

I will set nothing wicked before my eyes.

Psalm 101:3 NKJV

32. <u>Waking Up Depressed on Sundays</u>

(By Karen Joy King)

Many years ago, I would wake up with a cloud of depression over me on Sundays. Finally, I asked the Lord why. (Duh! Why did it take me so long?) He quietly asked me, "What TV programs have you been watching Saturday nights after the 11:00 p.m. news?" I thought for a little bit and then named the two programs.

He, in His faithfulness, showed me the "why" was in these particular programs ". . . <u>But God</u>!" Because of the ungodly content being aired through them, they opened the door for satan to attack me, not only Sunday mornings with depression but also throughout the night. I repented for watching these programs and never watched them again. And guess what? After that, I no longer wake up depressed Sunday mornings.

Later on, God showed me other TV programs, although the nature of them wasn't as bad, that I should no longer watch. At first, it was difficult for me to give some of them up, but because I wanted to obey God, I did and have been glad ever since that I did.

For years, I have been very careful about what I watch realizing that whatever I put before my eyes is going to affect me in many ways. I want to keep my eyes pure so my whole body will be pure and holy unto God since He dwells within me and my body is His temple. (Psalm 101:3) (I Peter 1:16)

Then David said to Saul,
"Let no man's heart fall because of him; your
servant will go and fight with this Philistine."

I Samuel 17:32 NKJV

33. <u>David and Goliath</u>

<u>(Paraphrased from I Samuel 17)</u>

(By Karen Joy King)

This is a very familiar story to many, but I think it has earned its place in ". . . <u>But God</u>!" as a good review that with God nothing is impossible and that it pays to run at any giant in our lives with our mouths open. The story:

Israel was at war again with their enemy, the Philistines, only this time, the Philistines had a champion warrior, a huge giant by the name of Goliath. Day after day, while the army of Israel hid in the bunkers, the giant would taunt them, "Why do you come out to battle and not fight? Am I not the Philistine and you servants of King Saul? Choose a man for yourselves and let him come and fight me, if he is able to do so. If he kills me, you win, and we will serve you; if I kill him, you will become our servants." I can imagine that the giant would laugh raucously after his threats and taunts, which only put more fear into King Saul and his army.

A young man by the name of David was a shepherd who grew up tending his father's sheep. During his long, lonely days in the fields, he learned to trust and love God. There were many dangers while in the fields for bears and lions would often come to kill the sheep. David had a lot of time to practice with his only weapon, a slingshot. With it, coupled with his trust in God, he had killed numerous large ferocious animals.

Since David's older brothers were in Saul's army, David's father told David to take them some food and to check on their welfare. When David arrived at the battle ground, he heard the taunts of the giant and saw the fear of the Israelite army. David became very angry seeing that no one would fight Goliath while continuing to allow him to taunt God's army. David went to King Saul and said, "Let no one be discouraged because of this giant. I will go and fight him."

Saul and the army thought there was no way this young strapling could do this. But David replied, "I was tending my father's sheep when a lion or a bear came and took a lamb from the flock, I went out after him and attacked him, and rescued the lamb from his mouth; and when he rose up against me, I grabbed him by his beard, struck him, and killed him. I have killed both the lion and the bear, and this wicked Philistine will be like one of them, since he has taunted the armies of the living God."

"The Lord, who delivered me from the paws of the lion and the bear, will deliver me from the hand of this Philistine." Notice David's words – he was proclaiming victory before attempting to do battle with the giant. We need to do the same thing – open our mouths before we attempt to fight a battle and proclaim the victory – out loud. In order to be able to do this, we need to keep our mouths filled with God's Word and faith instead of words of defeat, despair, discouragement, and unbelief. Saul then told David, "Go, and may the Lord be with you."

David went out, found five smooth stones, put them in his shepherd's bag, took his staff and sling and headed toward the giant. When the giant saw David coming toward him, he said to David, "Am I a dog that you come against me with sticks (David had his shepherd's staff in his hand)? Then the giant began to curse David by his gods, and said to David, "Come to me, and I will give your flesh to the birds of the sky and the beasts of the field." The giant also made an out loud proclamation, but he didn't have God on his side like David did.

David said, "You come to me with a sword, a spear, and a javelin, but I come to you in the name of the Lord of hosts, the God of the armies of Israel, whom you have taunted and defied. This day, the Lord will deliver you into my hands. I will strike you down and remove your head. I will give the dead bodies of the army of the Philistines this day to the birds and the wild beast, that all the earth may know that there is a God in Israel, and that all this assembly may know that the Lord does not deliver by sword, or spear; for the battle is the Lord's, and He will give you into our hands."

Notice that David stood firm in God and proclaimed victory before it happened. This is a good example of how we should face our giants and battles. Face them with our mouths open proclaiming God's word and run

159

toward them in God's power instead of cowering and running away from them hoping that they will go away.

The giant rose up and came against David, but David ran to the giant, while putting one of his stones in his sling. He slung it and God guided it. The stone forcibly struck the giant in his forehead and caused him to fall on his face to the ground. David took Goliath's own sword and cut his head off, just as he said he would.

Notice another lesson here. Once David said he was going to kill Goliath, he didn't mess around or hesitate. He ran to finish the job before Goliath could counteract. Too many times, we lose the battle to our giants by procrastinating.

When the Philistine army saw their champion was dead, they fled. Now filled with renewed strength due to David's bravery, the army of King Saul pursued them. Israel slew the Philistine army and plundered their camps. It was a great day in Israel because a little shepherd boy didn't back down in the face of a giant. If you are willing to face your giants in the name of the Lord, God will help you kill them, too ". . .<u>But God</u>!"

All good things come to those who wait.

Abraham Lincoln

34. <u>Received a Husband and a House</u> <u>Through Prayer</u>

(By Karen Joy King)

I have an older friend who lost her husband to cancer in 1999. From the time I became acquainted with them, she and her husband seemed to be on a perpetual honeymoon since they were so much in love with each other. His death was devastating to her since they could hardly stand to be apart for more than ten minutes when he was alive. Both were wonderful, delightful people and dearly loved by many.

After many years of being alone, she began to pray for a husband, but with certain specifications. She wanted a man a little younger than herself; a man who would be from her church; and a man who wasn't poor. Keep in mind that when a person gets older, finding those who are available is very slim even without these specifications.

After several years of praying like this, a man from her church, who had lost his wife a couple of years before due to illness, asked my friend out. He was younger and by no means poor. (All three specifications met in this man.) They dated for a time, fell in love, and he asked her to marry him; but she was hesitant due to several reasons. One was where they would live since they both had their own homes. Back to prayer she went.

They decided to buy a different home to begin their new life together – a fresh start. They began to search for houses on the internet and found several very nice homes in a location they both liked. Again, my friend had certain specifications in mind for a house. The second house they looked at met all her specifications (his too) and the wedding date was set. My friend will be treated like a princess by her new husband since he is a prince of a man!

Talk about specific answers to prayer. This is certainly a ". . . .<u>But God</u>!" story. If you are praying for something specific which is not outside of God's will; hang in there, for God loves to answer specific prayers and to take delight in His children!

The Lord shall preserve you from all evil.

Psalm 121:7a NKJV

35. <u>God Kept Her Home</u>

(By Karen Joy King)

The story I am about to share here is about another one of my students which is totally amazing. I am so glad she applied the principles she learned through Christian Leadership University.

One Sunday morning while getting ready for church, she was feeling extremely uneasy about going, but she really wanted to go and to take her twins with her. She began to pray, "Please Lord, I am presenting the eyes of my heart to You. Why shouldn't the girls and I go to church this morning?"

The result was astounding. God gave her a vision of the girls and her walking toward the church when her ex-husband came roaring down the street in his truck, stopped it with a screeching halt, and got out. He pointed a gun at her and fired. Since she was carrying her Bible opened against her chest, the bullet pierced through it and penetrated her chest, but she was ok.

All of the sudden police were surrounding him. End of vision.

She was in shock but knew that they shouldn't go to church, so they didn't go that morning. She thanks God for His revelation given through the vision because she later found out that her ex-husband had definitely plotted to kill them that day. As a result of not seeing them near the church, he killed himself. By submitting her eyes to God and asking His counsel, she and her girls were saved. ". . . <u>But God</u>!"

And you shall know the truth
and the truth shall make you free.
John 8:32 NKJV

36. <u>God Knew the Truth</u>

(By Karen Joy King)

This is another student's ". . . <u>But God</u>!" story.

She had run up a debt on her credit cards of over $40,000 to pay for her ministry courses. In order to help her pay this debt, her husband got a job as a purchaser for a certain company. However, the job turned out to be a scam.

In the beginning, the company started to pay off the credit cards but then made the bank return the funds, which she don't know was legal to do! She called the police, who came and checked all the documentation. Seeing she was in good faith, they in turn got the FBI involved.

Later on, she was sued for failure to pay the credit companies even though she had called them to make them aware of the scam, but they were only interested in collecting her debt.

After several months, the credit card attorneys started harassing her and told her she should get a

lawyer. Needless to say, she and her husband were
on their knees praying the whole time because they
couldn't afford an attorney, much less pay off the debt.
By now, even the police had become mute. The couple
had no idea what to do and were at their wits end! Being
at wit's end is actually good because it gives God an
opportunity to show Himself strong in our behalf. Our
importunities turn into God's opportunities!

She went to a court hearing to get the $395 court
fees waived which they couldn't afford to pay. She
wasn't sure how things would go in court ". . . <u>But
God!</u>" gave her victory! Her fees were waived!

More months passed during which they kept praying,
searching, reading God's promises, and keeping their
trust in Him. The main scriptures which gave her hope
and courage were based on Luke 12:12 and Luke 21:15.
"The Holy Spirit will give me the right words to say at
the time I need to say them." (Personalized)

Since another court date was coming up, they
trusted that the truth would be revealed as they, the
police, and the FBI know it should be. They had a

complete document ready to present; but one month before her court date, she got a letter in the mail stating the case had been **DISMISSED**!!! Wow! Talk about God working in their behalf! That was another ". . . But God!"

God does exceedingly beyond what we can EVEN fathom! (Ephesians 3:20, 21) God rewards those who seek Him. (Hebrews 11:6) She stated, "I am here to proclaim that God lives and reigns Omnipotent! So whatever you may find coming against you . . .it will NOT prosper." (Isaiah 54:17)

Even though she and her husband had always been very close, that situation almost caused division between them. At first, they blamed each other and fought until they came to their senses and began to seek God. Getting into the word together SAVED them! The enemy wanted so much to divide and to destroy them! Seeking God gave them their first victory over the situation because God enabled them to clearly see how to work through the problems. By gaining this understanding, they were able to stand together in God's

Word against the scammers instead of each other. That was certainly another ". . . .<u>But God!</u>"

The most unexpected part was getting the dismissal letter since they had no indication of it coming ". . . <u>But God</u>!" They stood firm on God's truth and it vindicated them!

To top this all off, people began sending them cash gifts who had no idea of their situation. ". . . <u>But God!</u>" He is so good – all the time!

For as the heavens are higher than the earth,

So are my ways higher than your ways.

Isaiah 55:9 NKJV

37. <u>The Reunion</u>

(By Karen Joy King)

Being a pastor myself with a start up church, I know what it is to have to be creative when things don't go as planned. I also know how God supplies and works miracles when things look hopeless. The following story speaks to my heart.

A brand new pastor and his wife were assigned to their first ministry, which was to reopen a church (I also reopened my church after having been closed for five years). They arrived in early fall excited about their opportunities. (Oh the vibrancy of youth!) When they saw their church, it was very run down and needed much work (as was my church when I first got it). They set a goal to have everything done in time to have their first service on Christmas Eve.

They worked hard, repairing pews, plastering walls, painting, etc, and on December 18 were ahead of schedule and just about finished. On December 19 a terrible tempest -- a driving rainstorm hit the area and lasted for two days.

On the 21st, the pastor went over to the church. His heart sank when he saw that the roof had leaked (my church's roof also leaked), causing a large area of plaster about 20 feet by 8 feet to fall off the front wall of the sanctuary just behind the pulpit, beginning about head high (thank God, mine wasn't this bad).

The pastor cleaned up the mess on the floor, and not knowing what else to do but postpone the Christmas Eve service, headed home. On the way he noticed that a local business was having a flea market type sale for charity, so he stopped in. One of the items was a beautiful, handmade, ivory colored, crocheted tablecloth with exquisite work, fine colors and a cross embroidered right in the center. It was just the right size to cover the hole in the front wall.

He bought it and headed back to the church. By this time it had started to snow. An older woman running from the opposite direction was trying to catch the bus, but she missed it. The pastor invited her to wait in the warm church for the next bus 45 minutes later.

She sat in a pew and paid no attention to the pastor while he got a ladder, hangers, etc., to put up the tablecloth as a wall tapestry. The pastor could hardly believe how beautiful it looked and it covered up the entire problem area. Then he noticed the woman walking down the center aisle.

Her face was white as a sheet. "Pastor," she asked, "where did you get that tablecloth?" The pastor explained. The woman asked him to check the lower right corner to see if the initials, EBG were crocheted into it there. They were. These were the initials of the woman, and she had made this tablecloth 35 years before in Austria.

The woman could hardly believe it as the pastor told how he had just gotten the tablecloth. The woman explained that before the war she and her husband were well-to-do people in Austria. When the Nazis came, she was forced to leave. Her husband was going to follow her the next week. He was captured, sent to prison, and she never saw her him or her home again.

The pastor wanted to give her the tablecloth; but she made the pastor keep it for the church. The pastor insisted on driving her home. That was the least he could do.

The Christmas Eve service was wonderful and the church was almost full. The music and the Spirit were great. At the end of the service, the Pastor and his wife greeted everyone at the door and many said that they would return.

One older man, whom the pastor recognized from the neighborhood continued to sit in one of the pews and stare, and the pastor wondered why he wasn't leaving. The man asked him where he got the tablecloth on the front wall because it was identical to one that his wife had made years ago when they lived in Austria before the war and how could there be two tablecloths so much alike.

He told the pastor how the Nazis came, how he forced his wife to flee for her safety and he was supposed to follow her, but he was arrested and put in a prison. He never saw his wife or his home again all the 35 years between. The pastor asked him if he would allow him to take him for a little ride. They drove to the same house where the pastor had taken the woman three days earlier.

He helped the man climb the three flights of stairs to the woman's apartment, knocked on the door, and he saw the greatest Christmas reunion he could ever imagine. After 35 years of separation due to a table cloth, the man and wife were reunited " . . . <u>But God!</u>"

In all your ways acknowledge Him,

And He shall direct your paths.

Proverbs 3:6 NKJV

38. <u>God Supplied the New Roof and Siding</u>

(By Karen Joy King)

When I purchased the church (explained in story #41), I needed to have it insured, so I called four different insurance agencies to give me their coverage and prices. One of the agents shared this story about her church.

Her church is a small church with a membership list of around 75 but regular attendance is only 38. The church needed a new roof and siding, but their congregation didn't have the funds to pay for this. The church treasurer contacted various banks, but none would grant them a loan since the church was so small. Not knowing what else to do, the pastor and Board prayed about their need and left it in God's hands believing that He would not allow the roof to cave in on them.

Shortly after that meeting, one of the unlikeliest church members, an 82 year old gentleman, asked if he could meet privately with the church treasurer. They went off into a room together and the gentleman, Ed, asked if she could keep something just between them. She replied that she would to the best of her ability but might need to talk with the pastor and Board, depending on what he wanted. He agreed that would be ok. He told her that he wanted to provide all the money for the new roof and siding.

The treasurer about fell over backwards and could hardly believe what he was saying. She asked Ed how soon he could get the money to them. He said as soon as the bank opened Monday morning.

The treasurer ran this by the pastor and Board, which they thought would work, but they wanted a legal contract with Ed since he said he would loan the money to the church. Ed told them the loan was to be a 50 year loan, no interest, and with payments starting in 60 days. The treasurer said, "But, Ed, you won't live that long." To which he replied, "Yes, I know, and when I am deceased, the loan is to be written off free and clear." So with that, Ed and the church Board set up the loan.

But that is not the end of the story. Each Sunday, Ed placed enough money in the offering to cover the loan payments!

God is interested in our every need, but first we have to take our hands off and simply let God be God. Once this church had exhausted their means and gave the need to God, He worked and fully supplied ". . . But God!"

The righteous cry out, and the Lord hears,
And delivers them out of all their troubles.
The Lord is near to those who have
a broken heart
And saves such as be of a contrite spirit.
Many are the afflictions of the righteous,
But the Lord delivers him/her out of them all.

Psalm 34:17-19

39. <u>Does Jesus Care?</u>

(Intro and comments by Karen Joy King)

Many times we are faced with tragedies we do not understand. How many times have we heard it asked, "Why do bad things happen to good people?" As long as we live on this earth, life happens. Things happen. Sometimes good people make bad or wrong choices. Sometimes good people don't obey nor heed God's warning and plow ahead in their own stubbornness. Living in disobedience to God and His word opens the door wide open for demonic attacks which result in bad things happening to them.

Good people are living in a wicked and fallen world so to expect our lives to be untouched by evil is living with unreal expectations. However, God has promised to always be with us no matter what we face. He has promised to deliver us. "The righteous cry, and the Lord hears and delivers them out of all their troubles. The Lord is nigh unto them that are of a broken heart; and saves those who are of a contrite spirit. Many are the afflictions of the righteous; but the Lord delivers him out of them all." (Psalm 34:17-19)

This is a true story about a terrible tragedy that happened to a pastor at the turn of the 1900's. (From Nickel Notes as given by Sue Smith)

"When my mother was a little girl, she attended a Methodist Church in Philadelphia, PA, that was pastored by Frank E. Graeff. My mother did not remember him telling this story, but she DID remember HER mother relating this hymn story to her from their pastor.

Apparently, the Graeffs had a daughter who was a beautiful girl. She was a young lady at this time and as was the custom of the day, all girls and ladies wore floor-length dresses with many layers of lace or frills. Their homes were heated at that time with fireplaces or wood-burning stoves. One day, the daughter got too close to the fireplace and her long skirt caught on fire. They frantically tried to save her, but the fire consumed her so rapidly, nothing could be done. She was burned to death in the fire.

Pastor Graeff was overcome with grief, as you might imagine. Like many Christians often do when bad things happen to them, he began to question if Jesus really cared about this tragedy that had engulfed their family. When he turned to the Lord, the following words came to him:

'**Does Jesus care**, when I've said goodbye
To the dearest on earth to me?
And my sad heart aches till it nearly breaks-
Is it aught to Him? **Does He see?**'

As Pastor Graeff asked these questions and others of the Lord, he could hear the Lord answering him

'Oh,**YES, He cares**! I know He cares,
His heart is touched with my grief;
When the days are weary, the long nights dreary;
I know my Savior cares.'
'Does Jesus care when my heart is pained
Too deeply for mirth and song;

As the burdens press, and the cares distress,

and the way grows weary and long?'

'Does Jesus care when my way is dark

With a nameless dread and fear?

As the daylight fades into deep night shades,

Does He care enough to be near?'

'Does Jesus care when I've tried and failed

To resist some temptation strong;

When for my deep grief I find no relief,

Though my tears flow all the night long?'

'Oh, YES, He cares! I know He cares,

His heart is touched with my grief;

When the days are weary, the long nights

dreary;

I know my Savior cares.'

I am so thankful that we have these words to comfort us during time of affliction, even though the author had no idea what God was going to do during his time of grief. This is one of my favorite hymns, and it has comforted me many times throughout my life!

But the Lord was with Joseph
and showed him mercy,
And He gave him favor . . .

Genesis 39:21 NKJV

40. From a Prisoner to a Ruler (The Troublesome Coats)

(Paraphrased from Genesis 37, 39-50)

(By Karen Joy King)

One of my favorite Bible stories is about Joseph. Every time I read or think about his life, I know there is hope for me. And you can know there is hope for you from this story. No matter how bad our circumstances may be at the moment, God can lift us up into a much better situation if we will be true to Him and keep trusting Him. Along with this story, I want to share two quotes by Norman Vincent Peale which have also helped me when things get tough. "It is always too soon to quit." "Never doubt in the dark what you were told in the light."

Joseph was the favorite and most loved son of his father Jacob. Jacob made no bones about it either for he constantly gave Joseph nicer things than the rest of his eleven brothers, which caused them to hate him.

This is a good warning to parents to not favor one child above another because it causes much heartache within a family. Children can easily feel unwanted and unloved when a parent favors their siblings above them. Every son/daughter needs to be loved, valued, and made to feel special. Children need to be taught to honor and love one another.

One of Jacob's favors to Joseph was when he gave Joseph a beautiful coat of many colors. It represented Jacob's intense love for Joseph. It could have represented other things, too, since the actual meaning is disputed. Some say it could have been a robe with long sleeves or a coat with stripes or with pictures on it. At any rate, it was a special gift which represented royalty and love. This coat produced even more envy and hatred for Joseph from his brothers.

Joseph's Coat
Drawn by Heidi Smith

". . . <u>But God</u>!" was setting things in motion to fulfill His plan, for God had told Joseph's grandfather, Abraham, that his descendents would go to Egypt and be there 400 years as slaves. After this time, they would be delivered and brought to the land of their promised inheritance, Israel.

God gave Joseph some special dreams. In them, they showed his mother, father, and brothers bowing down to him. Joseph, being young and naïve, foolishly told these dreams to his brothers which caused them to hate him even more.

One day Jacob sent Joseph to check on his brothers who were tending the flocks of sheep in another area. When his brothers saw him coming, they conspired against him and plotted to kill him; however, his oldest brother tried to intervene in order to save Joseph's life. So instead of killing him, they stripped him of his colorful coat and sold him to a passing band of Ishmaelites, who carried him to Egypt and sold him to Potiphar, an officer of Pharaoh. At that time, Joseph was 17 years old.

Meanwhile, the brothers took Joseph's coat, dipped it in blood, and took it to Jacob. They let Jacob believe that Joseph had been killed by a wild beast. Because of Jacob's favoritism toward Joseph, now Jacob was deeply grieving the loss of his son and his brothers were living a lie.

Joseph, now a slave, worked faithfully for Potiphar, and God favored him. Potiphar put Joseph in charge of everything he had. As Joseph worked the estate,

Potiphar's wife saw how handsome he was and wanted to have an affair with him. Joseph continually resisted her advances, but one day when no one else was in the house, she cornered him insisting that he make love to her.

Joseph quickly fled; but as he did, she caught his coat (coats sure do cause problems for Joseph). When Potiphar came home, his wife lied to him about Joseph trying to take advantage of her. Evidently, there was no just trial because Joseph was immediately thrown into prison. His life was going from bad to worse, yet he did not blame God or have a pity party for himself.

God once again favored him, and Joseph was put in charge of the prison. He served there many years until Pharaoh had some dreams. Two years prior to Pharaoh's dream, two of Pharaoh's servants, the chief butler and chief baker, had angered him so he put them in prison. It was the same prison Joseph was in, so he helped tend to their needs.

Both the butler and baker each had a dream the same night, which troubled them greatly. When Joseph came the next day to tend to them, he asked them why they were so depressed. They shared their dreams. Joseph interpreted both their dreams and both dreams came to pass as Joseph had told them. The chief baker was hung, but the chief butler was restored to his position with Pharaoh. Joseph asked the butler to plead his case to Pharaoh since Joseph was innocent. Of course, the butler promptly forgot Joseph until Pharaoh had dreams no one could interpret.

Then the butler remembered how Joseph had correctly interpreted his dream and told Pharaoh about him. Pharaoh immediately called for Joseph to come. God gave Joseph the interpretation along with wisdom on how to handle what God was going to do to the world which God had shown Pharaoh in the dreams. There would be seven years of plenty followed by seven intense years of famine.

Pharaoh was so pleased and impressed that he made Joseph second ruler of Egypt. Joseph was set free and lifted up in minutes. God can do the same for us, so never think that your situation is impossible or taking too long. At the right time, God will lift you up, too ". . .But God!"

Because of the famine, Jacob sent Joseph's brothers to Egypt to buy food. While there, they bought food from Joseph, whom they did not recognize. They bowed down to him as ruler of Egypt. Joseph's dream had come to pass and so were God's words to Abraham. Joseph later revealed himself to his brothers and had his father, brothers and their families all move to Egypt, just as God told Abraham they would.

After Joseph had died and a Pharaoh rose to power who didn't know Joseph, the Israelites, as they came to be called were forced into slavery. For 400 years they served under harsh task masters until God brought them out by Moses.

After they left Egypt and were on their way to the Promised Land, Israel, instead of being grateful that they did not have to be slaves anymore, they repeatedly disobeyed God, revolted against Him, and constantly complained. As a result, they had to wander in the wilderness for 40 years instead of making the trip in 11 days as they should have if they had obeyed God. Many were killed outright by God during this time because of their murmuring and complaining. After Moses had died, Joshua finally led the Israelites into their promised land, as God had promised.

Whenever we complain, we grieve God and suffer grave consequences. God doesn't kill us like He did the Israelites, but we don't receive God's best. So be like Joseph and serve God with a true heart in whatever circumstances you are in without complaining, griping, murmuring, or getting angry with God and wrongfully blaming Him. Joseph flourished in God's timing, but the complaining, ungrateful Israelites died and did not inherit the Promised Land.

Moreover whom He predestined,

these He also called;

Whom He called, these He also justified;

And whom Hew justified, these

He also glorified.

Romans 8:30 NKJV

41. This Was Not in My Plans – Not in a Million Years!

(By Karen Joy King)

One of the churches in Fayette, Ohio had been closed for five years. Since it is only a block from my house, I could see it through my window and would pass it when going up town. The old, original part had been built in the late 1800's, which a fire had destroyed, but it was rebuilt again in the 1920's.

Around the 1960's, it closed and another denomination bought it. A young pastor and his wife were called to pastor it. My mother started attending and later my youngest brother. This pastor was there three years and left. At that time, my husband and I were called to pastor it. We were there three years and left.

The church had several pastors through the years and then the first pastor returned. By this time, the church had grown significantly. A church school was added along with a new addition. My father and brother helped in the construction, along with many others, and it was completed in 1989.

After that, several more pastors came and went until the church dwindled and closed in 2007. The longer the church set empty, the more I was bothered. So every time I thought about it or went by it, I prayed a little prayer something like this. "Father, please bring someone along to buy the church and raise it up for Your glory. Make it a place where people can come in and hear the pure Gospel preached, a place where people can get saved, filled with the Spirit, and then minister to others."

I also wanted to attend there so I could walk to church. Since I have been in various forms of ministry over the years, I basically wanted to retire, just attend, and sit on the back pew! Yeah! Right! God has a sense of humor as you will find out in the following paragraphs!

I prayed that prayer until 2012 when one day as I was praying it, God gave me a very clear vision of a great big Jesus standing on the west side of the church,

placing one hand on it, and breathing His breath into it.
This made me very excited because it looked like there
was something about to happen with that church.

New Beginnings Ministries of Fayette, Ohio

Every time I continued to pray my little prayer, now I
also saw the vision. This went on for a couple of days when
the vision changed. Jesus picked up the church and gave
it to me. When I realized what this meant, I emphatically
kept saying, "No, no, no!!!!! I can't do this!!!!!!"

Immediately, in the vision, Jesus came behind me
and placed His arms and hands under mine, supporting
me holding the church. From that point on, Jesus and I
had many, many conversations until one day in April,

He told me in no uncertain terms to go buy the church. I obeyed Him.

That summer I spent every day working in and outside the church. Since it had been neglected for so long, it needed a lot of repair and cleaning. I enjoyed this time alone with God, communing with Him, and getting to know every nook and cranny in and around the place. It gave me quiet time with God, which I needed, to process this new calling – that of starting up the church and pastoring it.

The first Sunday I stepped in the church to have my own little worship service, God met me so powerfully, I could not move. All I could do was to raise my hands in praise and worship to Him. I bawled like a baby for quite some time, but they were tears of blessing and confirmation! God and I had a great time together that Sunday!

When people found out that I had bought the church and saw activity there, they were very encouraging and affirming. God began to bring others to help with cleaning, fixing, and providing financial support.

On Saturday, August 11, during a work day, five different people asked me when I would open for services. I told them I met there Sundays at 10:30 a.m., and they were welcome to join me. Seven people came Sunday, August12th, and we have been having services ever since. I had not planned on opening this soon ". . . But God!" had other plans, and He is blessing us!

You just never know what God may call you to do next! Be open and obedient and God will bless you beyond your wildest imagination! I thought I was getting too old to keep going like I was, ". . . But God!" reminded me that He didn't call Moses until he was 80 years old

At the time of this book's completion, I am 65 years young! God calls me a "spring chick!" Like I said, He has a sense of humor. I was wanting to slow down, and then He gave me the church to pastor ". . . But God!" My life has done anything but slow down, but I am enjoying this new calling and am excited to see what God is going to do next!

Bring all the tithes into the storehouse,

That there may be food in My house.

And try Me now in this, says the Lord of hosts,

If I will not open for you the windows of heaven

And pour out for you such blessing

that there will not be room enough to receive it.

And I will rebuke the devourer for your sakes.

Malachi 3:10-11 NKJV

42. <u>She No Longer Worries About Her Bills</u>

(By Karen Joy King)

One Sunday morning after I had started the Worship Service, I asked for praise testimonies. After several congregants had testified, one lady stood up and related how difficult it had been for her to juggle her bills since her income wasn't that much. When she attended church, she would put whatever she might have with her in the offering plate -- a few $1's, or a $5, or maybe a $10, or once in a while a $20.

It wasn't until she changed churches that she learned about tithing the first ten percent off the top of her gross income. This seemed rather scary since it seemed like she needed every cent to pay her bills. Since she needed to see this in black and white, she sat down and made out a budget. She thought that if she could see this on paper it might make more sense.

When she wrote her budget, on paper it looked impossible to pay her tithe and her bills, so she started taking from the tithe to balance her expenditures. This simply was not working, so she wadded up the budget and threw it away! Finally, she decided she would obey God and put Him to the test; after all, He promised that He would open the windows of heaven and pour out a blessing until she could not contain and to rebuke the devourer for her sake, if she obeyed Him and brought her tithe to His storehouse. Finally, she said in resignation and obedience, "Ok, God, here goes!"

With much trepidation, she wrote her first tithe check and put it in the offering at church. Wow, amazingly, God stretched the 90% of her income and her bills got paid! She said, "I hardly think about it when I write out my tithe check now because just as God promised, He is blessing me! I no longer have to worry about paying my bills ". . . <u>But God</u>!" God honored her as He does anyone who obeys Him. Nothing is impossible for God!

"Will a man rob God? Yet you have robbed Me! But you say, 'In what way have we robbed You?' In tithes and offerings. You are cursed with a curse, for you have robbed Me, even this whole nation. Bring all the tithes into the storehouse, that there may be food in My house, and try Me now in this says the LORD of hosts, if I will not open for you the windows of heaven and pour out for you *such* blessing that *there will* not *be room* enough *to receive it.* And I will rebuke the devourer for your sakes. . . . says the LORD of hosts." (Malachi 3:8-11a)

For He shall give His angels charge over you,

To keep you in all your ways.

Psalm 91:11 NKJV

43. <u>An Angel Saved My Life</u>

(From Kary, brother of Karen Joy King)

Why is it that when a child (or anyone for that matter) when told not to do something, that is exactly what they want to do? For instance, when my sister was little, she was told not to stick her tongue on any metal during the winter. She was told her tongue would stick to it. So what does she do? Goes out and sticks her tongue on a metal corn picker setting in the yard.

Well, just as she was warned, her tongue stuck to the cold metal and it took her a few minutes to get herself freed. When she finally got her tongue unstuck, a few layers of skin had peeled off. Ouch! But she had learned her lesson – the hard way – and never tried that again.

I had a similar incident. Growing up on a farm, dad had a certain lot enclosed with hot electric wire and the current was set up so it was a steady high voltage. I had been warned to not touch that wire.

One day a neighbor boy came over to play with my sister and me. We were playing in that hot-wired lot. They were at one end, and for some reason I was at the other end. While playing, I accidently fell into some water which filled my boots. Since I was cold and wet, I wanted to go to the house and change. Forgetting about the live hot wire, I put both my wet gloved hands on it to climb over the fence.

The instant I put my hands on the wire, the current was so strong, I couldn't let go. Since I was wet, the current was very strong. I screamed for help knowing that my life was fast slipping from me. In fact, at that moment, I felt like I was breathing my last breath.

My sister and our friend ran as fast as they could to get to me but weren't close enough to reach me in time to save me. (Actually, it is a good thing they weren't close to me, for had they taken a hold of me, they too would have been electrocuted). It was then that I felt big strong hands take a hold of my shoulders and pull me free. My gloves were left hanging on the wire. There was no human near me so this was a ". . . <u>But God</u>!" moment when my angel came to my rescue and saved my life. I wish I could have seen him, but I do thank him for saving my life!

Gloves Stuck on Fence
Drawn by Heidi Smith

Yeah, though I walk through the valley
of the shadow of death,
I will fear no evil for You are with me.
Psalm 23: 4 NKJV

44. <u>Death Was Cheated</u>

(From Kary)

Many years ago, I worked at a factory in a small town in our area. I was needing a new burn barrel, so during my lunch break, I decided to take a torch out into the yard and cut the lid off from one of the many barrels which were no longer in use. It was a beautiful summer day, so I was in shirt sleeves. I didn't bother to put on safety glasses.

When I put the torch to the lid, the barrel exploded. The lid was blown over 325 feet away and the torch was forced back into my face. It was actually a good thing I didn't have the safety glasses on, or my injuries for this particular accident would have been much worse. It would have taken my eye out.

For a few moments, I was floating upward and was around a good 100 feet in the air when I looked down and saw my bloody, crumpled body on the ground. Then my ascension was stopped and was not allowed to go any higher. Suddenly, I was back in my body. I picked myself up, and knowing I needed help, stumbled back into the building. Even though I managed to get up and walk, I was in a state of shock and very stunned.

Once inside, my co-workers immediately laid me down because they thought I wasn't going to make it. A foreman knelt down and spoke into my ear, "Don't leave us! Don't leave us!" To which I replied, "I'm not going anywhere." The reason I knew that was because I had just been brought back from the dead.

An ambulance was called. They didn't think I would live long enough to take me to a hospital, so I was taken to a doctor's clinic on the other side of town. There, a doctor stitched up the large gash just above my right eye brow and cleaned the blood off my face. Before I left, I asked for a mirror but was refused. By the expression on his face, I knew I must not have looked too good.

I was driven from the clinic back to the industrial site where I was evaluated. Once that was finished they told me to go home and offered to drive me. I refused and said I could drive myself, which wasn't very smart.

It was only God's hand upon me that I managed to drive the twelve miles home; for by this time, my face was very swollen. When I entered my house, I went in somewhat backwards so my wife wouldn't see my face or my torn, bloody shirt.

She was surprised that I was home early. I told her I had a little accident and then turned around. She looked at me and about fell apart. She ran and threw her arms around me, clinging and sobbing.

For the rest of that day, because of her tender love and treatment to my face, I recovered very quickly and was able to go back to work the next day.

To this day, all I have left from that accident is a little scar just above my right eye brow when I should have been killed ". . . But God!"

Back to the explosion. It had been so loud and violent that it had been felt and heard all over the community. When I went back to a doctor, he told me that my ear drums should have been shattered, but my hearing hasn't been affected. Another ". . . <u>But God</u>!" Also, if the cutting torch had hit my face an inch lower, it would have taken out my eye. God is so good and faithful! He truly did walk through the valley of the shadow of death with me and brought me back to life that day!

We couldn't go forward; we couldn't go back
We needed the Lord to "part the Red Sea"
– and miraculously He did!

Ken Ham

45. <u>We Needed a Special Miracle</u>

(From AiG with permission)

If you have never heard of or visited the Creation Museum in Hebron, Kentucky, you need to put this place in your vacation plans. It is fascinating and Biblical! You can learn and see the truth of how God created this earth and experience all the wonderful exhibits displayed there. For me, this is exciting to share with you a little of the history and update of how God is working to continue to build this. May this encourage you as you read about the challenges and how God met them.

The latest project is to build an Ark Encounter outreach, but before explaining this, I will share with you one of AiG's letters, dated March 20, 2014, by Ken Ham, President of AiG. (He refers to God's miracles as "Red Sea" occasions, which fits as ". . . <u>But God!</u>" experiences.)

At Answers in Genesis (AiG) a few weeks ago, we were feeling a bit like the Israelites at the Red Sea as they were leaving Egypt. We couldn't go forward; we could go back. We needed the Lord to "part the Red Sea" – and miraculously He did!

In over 30 years of ministry, I have witnessed many "Red Sea" type occasions when we have stepped out in faith and then the Lord blessed the creation ministry. Before I get to the latest incredible miracle, here are just a few examples of the Lord's blessings over the years:

1. In order to go into full-time creation ministry in 1979, I needed to resign my position as a public science teacher in Australia. The growing creation ministry that had started in our house required my full-time attention. But there was no teacher to take my place.

The principal told me that my departure would leave the school and students in a terrible position regarding course work, exams, etc. So we prayed. Then, "out of the blue," a teacher called the school seeking a teaching job--the exact position I had. So I was able to resign and begin the ministry that many years later is known as Answers in Genesis.

2. At the beginning of our Australian creation ministry, we had no money to purchase books to sell at our lectures. Then Master Books, a creationist publisher in the U.S., agreed to sell us one large order. Because the owner back then only allowed one order per year, we realized we had to make a significant one: $20,000, which was huge for a small ministry. (Mally and I didn't tell the publisher we only had $200.)

But we trusted the Lord would provide. So we ordered this massive amount of books and asked our friends and family either to donate or loan us the funds so we could pay the bill. Eventually, we had raised all but $3000. It was almost time to pay the bill and we were praying for the remaining funds.

As we sat on our front porch talking about how we were going to find $3000, a man pulled up in his car. He said something like, "I have been burdened to help you get this ministry under way. My wife and I want to help you – so here is a check." The check was for $3000 ". . . But God!" (By the way, the publisher was so impressed, he let us place more than one order a year. Distribution of creation books began in a big way in Australia!)

3. At another time in the Australian ministry, we desperately needed a vehicle to travel to speaking events around this huge country. It needed to be a vehicle large enough to carry hundreds of books and some equipment. Well, we found a suitable, used vehicle for $11,000— but we simply had no money. We held a prayer meeting in our rented office and asked the Lord to provide this vehicle somehow. And then the phone rang. A supporter said he was burdened to give us a donation and asked if we had any specific needs. We told him we were just then praying for a much needed vehicle. He gave us the $11,000! ". . . But God!"

Over the years we've experienced many such special miraculous events. I must admit, the Lord has used those times of uncertainty to increase our faith—and I can see why! These faith steps, bathed in prayer, have become bigger and bigger over time!

When we first stepped out in faith in the 1990's to announce that AiG would be building the Creation Museum in northern Kentucky, we experienced a number of "Red Sea" or (". . . <u>But God!</u>" experiences as they are called in this book) challenges. When we lost the zoning approval for the original property we sought for the museum, <u>the Lord provided a far better piece of land</u>—and in a much better location.

Also, as the media covered the museum's rezoning and opposition by humanists, and as donors started to support the project, we enlarged the vision. We ended up building a much larger museum—which is now having a much bigger impact than we ever imagined.

Then, just before the museum opened in 2007, we had a massive problem—which could have actually stopped the Creation Museum from opening. Because we had been building the museum as we raised donations, and we were now in the final construction stage and trying to finish all of the exhibits at the same time, we had a severe cash flow problem.

If we didn't have considerable funding in advance for the final construction contracts, the museum opening would have to be cancelled. The local banks we had dealt with over the years were not willing to help. And we couldn't guarantee them that the remaining funds would come in through donations (even though we had shown for several years the Lord was providing).

Then a local bank, with a Christian board of directors, heard about our problem. They visited us and immediately arranged to help with the cash flow problem. You probably have never known this, <u>but we were within two days of actually cancelling the grand opening of the Creation Museum</u>. But then the Lord provided ". . . <u>But God!</u>"

Recently, we experienced another "Red Sea" miracle . . .

Once again, we have stepped out in faith to build a full-scale, evangelistic Noah's Ark in a project called Ark Encounter. We want people to come and have an encounter with Noah's Ark, and in so doing, have an encounter with God's Word—and with Jesus Christ.

America's Research Group has forecast that the annual attendance will be 1.2 to 2 million guests (depending on the economy at the time) with up to 60% of those guests being unchurched or infrequent church attendees. The Lord has burdened us to build Noah's Ark as a sign—a reminder—to the world that God's Word is true, and that the gospel in His Word is true.

As with the Creation Museum, we've had many struggles along the way, including massive attacks by atheists and some in the secular media—all aimed at trying to hurt or stop the Ark.

Phase One of the Ark Encounter, with a full-size Ark, is estimated to cost $73 million. Answers in Genesis has committed to raising around $29 million in donations (about $14 million of this has been raised so far). The rest of the funds were to come from a bond offering.

Now let me tell you about that bond offering. The account will astound you.

It's a long and complicated story. You see, there were some very deliberate misrepresentations and untruths published about the bond offering, including by an influential financial news outlet. It led to major complications that almost shut down the bond offering and the project. (We were restricted from responding to the media during the bond offering).

We had ample registrations for the bond offering, indicating tremendous interest in the Ark bonds that likely would have seen all of the bonds being sold. But brokerage firms—who had originally told us they would allow the purchase of the Ark bonds for their clients— began reversing their position after the negative media coverage of the Ark bond. This massive exodus forced the bond underwriter and trustee to set up a different method by which our supporters could purchase the bonds, all of which made acquiring the bonds much more challenging.

As a result, a number of people found it very difficult and complex to participate in the bond offering. We were at another "Red Sea" moment. AiG was within a week of the closing date for the bond offering—and we were several million dollars short of the minimum amount needed for the bond closing (and facing the horrible prospect of having to refund all the bond funds held in escrow). From a human perspective, the project was in great jeopardy.

<u>But because we were convinced God had called us to build the Ark Encounter, and we had seen His miraculous hand so many times along the way, we believed that God would somehow bless this massive faith step we had taken—so we called people to pray.</u>

Now in God's providence, looking back we can see His miraculous hand in circumstances that led to a "parting of the Red Sea".

1. The debate between Bill Nye "the Science Guy" and me in February, that went viral around the world, occurred in God's providence right

before the bond closing. Now, registrations for the bond offering had already closed by the time of the debate, but a number of people who had already registered for the bonds, but who had not yet moved forward to fill out the complex paperwork, became so enthused by the debate that they worked extra hard to overcome the seemingly insurmountable difficulties. The debate encouraged them to ensure their participation and make the bond offering successful.

2. A number of AiG supporters who were bond holders were shocked by the media attacks, so they decided to increase their participation in the bond offering.

3. Others who knew about the bond problem helped in ways we did not think possible. So we were several million dollars short of the minimum amount for the bond and were within a week of the closing date. Millions in bond

funds in escrow might have to be returned. But God "parted the Red Sea". We can now begin to walk across! <u>Construction of the Ark Encounter will now get underway</u>. What a blessing!

In addition to what has been raised in donations for the Ark Encounter so far, AiG's goal is to raise $15 million more in donations to provide the funding for the special high-tech and interactive exhibits that guests have come to appreciate at the Creation Museum.

Karen King's note: I don't get paid for any of this, but if you'd like to help AiG reach that goal by making a gift of any size to the Ark Encounter project—consider sponsoring a peg, plank or beam in the Ark for you, family, or a friend.

You can also support the Ark Encounter by obtaining a lifetime membership (called Boarding Passes) as an individual or for your family. There are also other ways to help fund this worthy project. If you would like to do so, please contact AiG.

Address: POB 510, Hebron, KY 41048-0510

Phone: 859-727-2222

Fax: 859-727-2299

Internet: www.answersingenesis.org

The last note Ken Ham added was:

Please rejoice with us for the miraculous blessing we just experienced with the Ark bond! This incredible project will reach millions of souls with the truth of God's Word and the gospel of Jesus Christ.

"For I know the plans I have for you,"
declares the LORD, "plans to prosper you
and not to harm you, plans to give you
hope and a future."

Jeremiah 29:11 NKJV

46. <u>God Has a Plan for My Life</u>

(From Ryan)

Before I made my fresh start with God, I was going down a path of self-destruction. I did not have much direction as to what I wanted to do with my life other than to live for myself.

I made a game plan for my life, or so I thought, that I would be a professional baseball player. ". . . <u>But God</u>!" had a different plan for me. He sent one of his angels to me to help get me on the right path. Little did I know at the time that the angel would be the person I ended up marrying.

My wife, Jocelyn, witnessed to me one night and told me the importance of having Jesus Christ in my life. She then invited me to Bethany Assembly of God. There I started to hear and receive truth and saw that what I was doing at the time was not going to get me where I wanted to go in life.

From the Bible, I read that God has a plan for me, a plan to prosper me, and to give me a future. I realized that if I gave my life to Him that I would live a fruitful life. I am thankful to have received the message of Jesus Christ and to now know Him as my Savior!

God has blessed me by surrounding me with people who are living their life through His glory and going out and spreading the good word. If God would not have changed my life, I would not be where I am today, and I would have not been given the wonderful, joyous life I live today ". . . <u>But God</u>!"

Epilogue

I could go on and on with many more stories for they are endless, just like our God Who is limitless; but I think you get the idea of how God is ready to meet your needs when you call upon Him. As some of these stories bear witness, God answers before a person can call upon Him for help, especially if they are asleep.

Anyone can have this kind of help, protection, and relationship with God if they acknowledge they are a sinner, repent of their sins, and invite Jesus into their hearts. When they do that, they become born again; born into a new family – the family of God!

As a son or daughter of God's family, we become heirs of God and joint-heirs with Jesus Christ. This means that everything God has (which is everything good), becomes ours. We just need to learn how to walk in all His promises, claim them by faith, and watch God work them out in our behalf.

Just as we are saved by faith, we need to continue to walk by faith. "For everyone who calls on the name of the LORD will be saved." (Romans 10:13) (Acts 2:21) "For we live by believing and not by seeing." (2 Corinthians 5:7) "And without faith it is impossible to please God, because anyone who comes to him must believe that he exists and that he rewards those who earnestly seek him." (Hebrews 11:6)

Learning to walk by faith with God consists of learning to hear His voice (see Appendix), being obedient to Him, reading and meditating on His Word, the Bible, talking with Him (praying), and attending a good Bible believing church where the Word of God is rightly divided. It means finding good Christian friends with whom to associate.

Unsaved, or ungodly friends, will hinder you and cause you to stumble in your Christian walk. However, once you accept Jesus as your Lord and Savior and your life is changed, those kinds of friends may drop you. But having Jesus as a close Friend is the Best Friend you can ever have, as you have read in these ". . . But God!" stories.

If you don't know Jesus, I invite you to please accept Him now. You can do so by praying this simple prayer and meaning it.

"Dear Jesus,

I have sinned against You and I am truly sorry. Please forgive me, take my life, and make it all You want it to be. Come into my life and be my Lord and Savior! Take over! Thank You! Amen!"

Now, fill in these blanks as a record to being born into God's family.

Name: _____ Date: _____

Add your testimony here:

Appendix

In order to hear God, we need to practice what the Psalmist told us in Psalm 46:10, (expanded version) "Be still, cease striving, let go, relax, and know that I am God." Also in Habakkuk 2:1,2, we are given another outline of connecting with God, "I will stand upon my watch, and set myself upon the tower, and will watch to see what He will say to me, and what I shall answer when I am corrected. And the Lord answered me, and said, 'Write the vision, and make it plain upon tablets, that he may run that reads it. For the vision is yet for an appointed time.'"

From these scriptures, we can see that we cannot hear from God unless we are still and ceasing from our striving. How hard it is to achieve this stance at times. At the moment, it might feel better to throw a fit, complain against God, wallow in our misery, have a pity party, and demand instant relief. But when we allow ourselves to do that, and if we allow such actions to continue, it becomes a habit, a way of life, and a demonic stronghold. Life will not be pleasant for us nor those around us. If this is the way you act, humbly come to God, repent, and ask His forgiveness. Then each and every day seek His strength to help you break this ungodly habit and replace it with good habits.

At first, this will be difficult, for bad habits aren't broken easily. With God's Spirit within us, if you have accepted Christ as your Lord and Savior, He is all powerful and can deliver you from whatever your need is. "For greater is He Who is in you than (the devil) who is of the world" (I John 4:4b)

All of God's fullness dwells in us but we need to learn to how release it and live a good Spirit-filled life. As we continue to look to God, His power will be released through us, and we can live victorious lives. "For whoever is born of God overcomes the world (bad habits, strongholds, etc.). And this is the victory that has overcome the world—our faith. Who is he who overcomes the world, but he who believes that Jesus is the Son of God." (I John 5:4, 5)

If you will stay focused on God, keep everything committed to Him, He will fight your battles and you won't have to, which is a much better way to live. God tells us in Exodus 14:14, "The Lord will fight for you, and you shall hold your peace." In other words, if you will stay still, remain at peace, and relinquish the struggle, the Lord will take over so the battle is no longer yours but the Lords. He will fight it for you, but you have to let Him.

I used to struggle very hard to be a Christian, and as a result I was miserable -- without peace, joy, and victory. When I became a student at Christian Leadership University and took the first course "Communion with God," my life was a total mess. (I am not being paid to "brag" about Christian Leadership University). I have included some of my experience below. This is the same testimony that is shared on Christian Leadership University's website.

God Delivered Me From My 20 Year Tunnel!

As a child, I was fortunate to have a family who attended church on a regular basis. At church, I enjoyed hearing the Bible stories and singing the little Sunday School choruses. These caused me to want to know God better and to give my life in service to Him.

As a young child, I gave my life to Christ but made it official at the age of 13 by acknowledging Christ publically and being baptized. However, the church didn't teach how to live victoriously as a Christian. I hungered to know much, much more.

Eventually, God led me to a church, in which I developed a very close walk with God and enjoyed having a wonderfully anointed ministry. After awhile, a divisive spirit came into the church, through which many lives, families, and marriages were ruined, mine included.

Due to years of adverse, abusive situations, and erroneous Biblical teachings, I suffered a complete health break down in 1982. I was so sick, the team of doctors working with me, couldn't figure out how I still managed to live ". . .But God!" knew! After the break, I slept continuously, almost around the clock, for about four months. I was also confined to bed for many years due to the extreme illness and weakness.

During those years and the ones that followed, I could hardly do anything but slowly started gaining some strength. Due to being so ill for many years, I no longer enjoyed the prayer life I previously had, nor was I able to meditate on God's word and have it become Rhema (God speaking His word into my heart on a personal basis) like it constantly did before my break. Needless to say, I was too ill and weak to attend church or to work. After my break, everything became dark and hopeless, and I entered into, what I call, my 20 year tunnel.

Besides suffering from being so ill, no one gave me help or encouragement. I felt totally abandoned and took my focus off God. Unfortunately, due to my mind constantly rehearsing my bad circumstances instead of standing on God's Word, I became very angry, bitter, and experienced the gamut of negative, ungodly emotions. With all that accumulated spiritual "junk" in my life, I could no longer pray. Oh, I tried but it only added more frustration and anger. I also tried to fast and to meditate on the Word, but since I was bound up in my ungodly emotions, I stayed in my tunnel and bondage. Once in a while, I would see a little light in that tunnel which would give me a glimmer of hope, only to have it extinguished time and again.

Finally, after 20 years of struggling to regain a close, victorious relationship with God once again but without success, one night I threw my hands into the air and told God that if He wanted me to be a Christian, He was going to have to take over and do it through me, for I couldn't do this anymore. I was tired of trying! I was done! At that point, God rejoiced and said, "Finally, now I can help you!" What a blessed place at which to finally arrive for now God could take over and lead me to victory since **I** was out of the way. My deliverance had started but it didn't come overnight.

Shortly after that surrender, a friend suggested that I go back to school and earn a Master's degree in Counseling. God, through her, planted a seed. After praying about this for a couple of months, I felt this was something God wanted me to do. So, every day, all day long for two whole weeks, while constantly praying, I searched the internet for the right university. None of the hundreds of universities I researched interested me.

After the two weeks of searching, I prayed once again, "Father, **if** You want me to do this, show me the right school -- **now**." (I was tired of looking and was beginning to wonder if I should do this after all.) I went back on line. Immediately, Christian Leadership University came up. I hadn't seen it before but it caught my attention. When I read the CLU catalogue, I knew beyond a shadow of a doubt this was the university through which to earn my Masters degree in Christian Counseling.

By faith (since I had been too ill for so many years to work a steady, decent job, my income was very low), I signed up for a Masters in Christian Counseling. This program promised to minister to me first, which I was craving. I knew that I needed help before I could help others.

Mark Virkler, founder and President of Christian Leadership University, called to welcome me as a CLU student. Before the conversation ended, not only was

I signed up for a Masters but also a Ph.D. in Christian Counseling at a price I could afford! I was soaring, rejoicing, and praising the Lord!

Since I was so excited and wanted to share this with someone, I immediately called my pastor to let him know. Immediately, he threw "ice water" on me by warning me against this and trying to talk me out of it. When I hung up, I was totally deflated; but instead of entertaining the doubts, I reviewed all God had worked out for me and was again reassured that this was God's will. This time, I rejoiced even more. Needless to say, I soon left that church.

During my first course, *Communion with God*, God began to remove the many years of hurt, frustration, anger, unforgiveness, bitterness, etc. through learning to do the two-way journaling, visions, and dreams. He showed me how much He loved me and wanted to help me.

The course was a great help and encouragement as I walked through it with Jesus and applied it to my life. After that, I took *Counseled by God*, which strengthened me even more and led me into a deeper relationship with Him. By this time, I loved hearing Him speak to me through the journaling and seeing Him in the visions!

After *Counseled by* God, I took *Prayers That Heal the Heart*. While the first two courses were so uplifting and such a blessing to go through, I hit a "brick wall" when I started *PTHTH*. Every lesson was a **BIG** struggle, but I was determined to be set free and knew that satan was fighting.

Since I was entrenched with so many strongholds, I knew I needed a counselor to help me, but not just any counselor. I needed someone who understood the PTHTH deliverance/counseling process as was taught in my courses because this type of counseling really changes lives rather than just "putting a Band-aid on an infested sore" like secular counseling does. Unfortunately many Christian Counselors don't understand this deliverance process either.

While explaining my difficulties and needs to Mark Virkler, he offered to do the deliverance/counseling with me (his place was a nine hour drive from my place). At first, I didn't want to go that far; was scared to death to go through this process; and embarrassed for anyone to know my deep problems; but I knew I couldn't continue life as I was. Finally, I decided to put the fears aside and get help.

The original four hour session Mark had offered to do with me turned into an all day event since I had so many issues. Mark went through the "Contributing Strands Worksheets" I had started. There was a big stack of them—one for each issue. One by one, each issue was addressed by allowing the Holy Spirit to show me my heart's need and then to direct the process for my healing.

During this time, even though God gave me wonderful journaling and visions and we had prayed through the deliverance prayers, nothing seemed any different. I felt the same as when I had come and big-time disappointment started to overcome me. But then I immediately began to shake this off by reminding the Lord and myself that I had driven all this distance and even though I felt no different, I was expecting deliverance and healing. By faith I claimed it!

While driving home the next day with a friend who had gone with me and was sharing the things God had shown me during the deliverance session, it happened! I suddenly saw with my spiritual eyes the top of my tunnel burst open, God's glorious light shine in, and His hand picking me up out of the tunnel. At that moment, He told me that I was set free from all my issues which had stemmed from the generational sins/ curses, ungodly soul-ties, negative expectations, inner vows, sin, and scenes without Jesus. I would never be in a tunnel again for He had work for me to do. I became a new woman and have been enjoying life outside the tunnel ever since.

After I completed my Masters degree, Mark Virkler asked if I would like to be a professor for CLU. Before Mark had called, God had already been speaking to me about renewing my calling as a teacher, only this time, my classroom would be without walls (I have students from around the world). I had not been able to teach for quite a while due to my poor health, but when this opportunity arose, I knew this was God calling me back into teaching.

I have a wonderful, personal relationship with Him and enjoy ministering in the callings God has given me as the CLU professor and pastor. Now, I enjoy and am blessed when my students and parishioners are set free from their bondages! God is so good and faithful! He will set anyone free who seeks Him! ". . . But God!"

Why did I include the above testimony? To show that God desires and has made provision to set everyone free who wants to be; and that He wants us to have a good life—a life that is blessed, victorious, and enabled to do His will. In order to find that, I had to be willing to be still, let go of my struggles, to cease from striving, to relax, and let God guide me. As I learned to follow the four steps as presented in Habakkuk 2: 1,2, I learned how to be in constant fellowship with God.

The four steps to learn to hear and see God can be used by anyone. They are as follows:

1. Be still (I will stand at my guard post)

2. Focus on Jesus (I will keep watch and see)

3. Tune to spontaneity (What He will speak to me)

4. Two-way journaling (Then the Lord said, 'Record the vision'

Many people journal to God and record their thoughts, activities of the day, etc., but that's it – a one-sided conversation. But did you know that God wants to have a dialogue with you – all the time? He constantly wants to reveal His love to you, guide you in your daily activities, give you wisdom and advice, comfort you when you hurt, and show you a better ways of doing things.

You can allow Him to do this by learning how to do the two-way journaling by simply using the four keys above and then by writing down your question or statement. As you wait quietly upon Him, write down His flowing, spontaneous thoughts to you. In faith, write down whatever comes to you and then check it against the principles in His Word, the Bible. It is also good to show your journaling to some good Christian friends so they can verify you are hearing from God. I have included some of my beginning journal entries below so you can get an idea of how to do it.

1. "Father, what do You want to say to me today?"

   "Karen, My Dearest and Beloved Child, I love you! I want to teach you more about abiding in Me and how to rest in Me!"

2. "Father, I love You and want to please You in all my ways. What do You want to say to me today?"

   "Karen, I know your heart's desire is to please Me and to reach others for Me, and I am well pleased! Remember, the greatest thing you can do is to believe in Me and to live out of My flow (divine initiative). It is not doing, but being. It is staying focused on Me, resting in Me, and not struggling in your own strength. Trust Me to open the right doors and to enable you to walk through them."

   "My Child, you are My chosen vessel so just keep resting in Me and enjoy Me."
   "Thank, You, Father!"

3. "Father, I am reading in Matthew about the Pharisees and certainly don't want any of their traits in my life. Please show me anything that is not You."

"Karen, My Beloved Daughter, you please Me greatly and are open to Me. You are quick to obey. Your heart is clean and righteous. Continue as you are and stay open to My voice."

4. "Father, I liked the definition I heard about grace the other night. Grace doesn't see who I am now but who I can become through You. I know by this world's standards, I am considered an old lady, but how do You see me through Your grace?"

"You shall inherit the nations as you have asked. You shall be My Ambassador to the world and shall have a mighty, powerful ministry. That which you don't finish in this life's phase, you shall continue throughout all eternity."

"But I thought everyone and everything will be perfect in heaven."

"Heaven is perfect, but don't forget about the 1000 year reign on earth. There will be much work to be done during that time. When that is over, you will continue to perform many wonderful tasks in heaven and be delighted greatly."

"I am unlimited. Eternity is unlimited and every moment in your eternal home with Me will be more blessed and wonderful than you can imagine."

"You are My anointed. Just like Gideon who proclaimed himself weak and a nothing, I called him My mighty vessel through whom I could accomplish My will and deliverance for Israel. See yourself as that – My mighty, anointed vessel through whom I will accomplish much."

"Here I am! Take me and fulfill Your will through me!"

5. Thank You, Jesus, for shedding Your blood for me so I can be set free from all oppression and bondage! What do You want to say about that?"

"Dearest Karen, I came so that you would have abundant life in everything – health, wealth, ministry, relationships, etc. Shake off the bondages of the past and look forward, for I will give you great favor and anointing. You are entering a new phase in which I will bless you, exceedingly, abundantly above all you can think or ask. You are My representative, My Ambassador to the world."

"Don't be afraid to move forward in My grace. Look ahead and see the mighty things I want to do through you. My Hand is upon you. Do not be afraid or dismayed. Do not focus on yourself but on Me at all times."

* *

You, too, can hear God like I did above for He personally wants to speak to you. Use the Four Keys I have given you so you can learn to hear His voice and dialogue with Him. Once you learn to hear Him speaking directly to you; telling you how much He loves you and how He wants to guide you, you'll never stop wanting to have this wonderful communion with Him! Enjoy your journey with God and experience some ". . . <u>But God's</u>!